Grace for the Journey

Grace for the Journey

Practices and Possibilities for In-between Times

Beverly A. Thompson
George B. Thompson, Jr.

 ALBAN

Herndon, Virginia
www.alban.org

The Alban Institute
2121 Cooperative Way, Suite 100
Herndon, VA 20171

Unless otherwise noted, all Scripture quotations are from the New Revised Standard Version of the Bible, copyright © 1989, Division of Christian Education of the National Council of the Churches of Christ in the United States of America, and are used by permission.

Cover Design by Signal Hill.

Library of Congress Cataloging-in-Publication Data

Thompson, Beverly.
  Grace for the journey : practices and possibilities for in-between times / Beverly A. Thompson, George B. Thompson, Jr.
    p. cm.
  Includes bibliographical references (p. 117).
  ISBN 978-1-56699-420-0
  1. Change--Religious aspects--Christianity. 2. Church renewal. 3. Possibility--Religious aspects--Christianity. 4. Communities--Religious aspects--Christianity. 5. Spiritual life--Christianity. I. Thompson, George B. (George Button), 1951- II. Title.
  BV4509.5.T4855 2011
  262.001'7--dc23
                        2011033771

11   12   13   14   15   VP   5   4   3   2   1

Contents

Foreword

It has become a cliché among pastors these days for us to get together and complain about all the things "they didn't teach us in seminary." Every gathering seems to tick off the same, very predictable list of stumbling blocks (usually centering on finances and program management), which is followed by an equally predictable list of solutions (required business and management classes). However, because this landscape has been trod many times, these technical problems are quickly eclipsed by a discussion of something deeper—something more fundamental to the life of the congregations we all serve.

What we pastors witness when the surface symptoms have been stripped away is a lack of imagination on both our part and on the part of the churches we serve. We know that no matter how many new skills we learn, the likelihood of achieving the kind of growth and vitality that our congregations desire is going to be small. When we're honest with ourselves, while we would certainly like to be more skilled at navigating finances or shepherding programs, we know that what our congregations need from us is something else. The issues we are facing will not be solved if we become experts at spreadsheet pivot tables. Finding a better way to track youth permission slips will not magically return us to the golden days of congregational life.

We know that what we need is the ability to play again. We need new lenses through which to view our lives. We need to find new landmarks to guide us in our work. But how, exactly, do we tap into the imagination we know is needed? Where do we find these new lenses? How do we gain a view of the landscape as it really is and not keep using the same maps to traverse the same terrain?

In the congregation I just finished serving, we found ourselves at a crossroads regarding our Christian Education programming. Everything seemed to be falling apart right before our eyes. Within the span of 18 months, the volunteer base we had always depended on seemed to vanish, various families began to have other commitments, and many in the congregation were of the mindset that all that was required was a hunkering down. If we did that, the glory days of well-attended fellowship dinners followed by a full slate of well attended classes would return. But the Education Committee knew better.

For six months we struggled through a process of discernment, of letting go of the past and mining the community for new sources of energy and gifts. It was a long process, and one that finally bore good fruit; but, as pastor, I found myself often cautioning against a quick-fix mentality. I believed that we might full well end up with a program that closely resembled the one we had just laid to rest, but the difference would be made in the quality of our imagination. But getting a group to believe me was a difficult task. There were several times during that process that I would have sold my birthright in exchange for guidance of how to bring the group along with me.

What you hold in your hands is the guidance I was looking for.

Beverly and George Thompson are painfully clear that the book you have picked up is not a "how-to manual." It might be discouraging for you to discover that nowhere in this book are you going to find a list of easy steps. But what you will find inside is something much richer.

In my book, *Open Source Church*, I made the case that congregations everywhere are facing a significant transition moment. The way to navigate this transition is not by calling in an expert of some sort who will give you the answers and take away your fears. Expertise, I contend, is surprisingly limited. Instead, the way forward is to draw upon the wisdom of the people God has gathered in each particular community. All of the wonderful people in our congregations are there for a reason. They each have a particular perspective, gift, or skill that will assist their community in navigating the uncharted waters they are facing. The important work is not one of producing the right content, but of finding the right process.

In *Grace for the Journey*, Beverly and George provide us with as good of a process as I have ever seen. Drawing on the conviction that Christians are people of practice, they are not satisfied just to give us new lenses through which to see our world. Beyond guiding us to discover beautiful new vistas, they offer us ways of integrating that beauty into the living of our lives.

So take heart. All is not lost. Beverly and George are correct: there is ample grace for the journey your congregation is on. God has not and will not leave you to perish in the wilderness. Just like the promise Abraham received, there is a new land for us to inhabit if we just have the faith to take the first step.

Landon Whitsitt
Vice-Moderator
219th General Assembly of the Presbyterian Church (USA)

Grace for the Journey

Introduction

First Church has been a mainstay of its small university town for more than 150 years. It was the place where college students congregated for food and fellowship in the '50s and '60s. Some of those students were married at First Church and continue to worship there today. Their kids grew up at First, went off to college, and moved away. First Church viewed itself as a thriving congregation where worship remained the central focus and longtime friendships were valued. The members of First Church were comfortable—until they began to notice that their Sunday school classrooms, once filled with the laughter of children, were now empty. Worship attendance is down; finances are stretched. The once highly prized sanctuary has a leaking roof, paint-chipped walls, and too many steps for some to navigate. First Church is beginning to feel empty and lifeless. Last Sunday, the pastor announced his retirement.

What will happen to this church and those who hold it dear?

How will this congregation choose to live in this in-between time?

Mill Creek Church sits on what was once a cornfield. Today, a small industrial area that includes a lumber mill and a building supply warehouse surrounds the church building. The remaining church members no longer live nearby, although a few had jobs at the lumber mill before times got rough. The church's pastor, Rev. Barker, works part-time at both the church and the supply warehouse. He is the congregation's fourth part-time pastor in the last ten years. The church has always had a heart for helping people, but in its struggle to survive, it has turned its focus inward. Declining membership, dwindling finances, and few visitors all serve to increase the congregation's anxiety. "We've always done it this way" rings loud and clear at every gathering.

The congregation is weary and listless. "Rev. Barker needs to get busy" is heard regularly in the church parking lot and at the local grocery store. But how can Mill Creek Church and its pastor focus on building their future, without getting into a blame game? Where might they turn their attention in order to gain new insight and energy?

The stories of these two congregations are echoed in mainline churches across the country. Is it possible to imagine that grace-filled possibilities await these two congregations? And what about your congregation? Can you imagine what you might discover in your church's in-between time?

> *Can you imagine what you might discover in your church's in-between time?*

Facing Transition

Throughout its lifetime, every community of faith journeys through periods of transition. As strange as it sounds, this is good news—not bad! Transitions are essential for thriving congregations, because these in-between times open us to new grace-filled possibilities. Of course, many transitions emerge out of some kind of crisis, so congregations often think of all transition as negative by definition. In reality, in-between time offers your community of faith a distinctive opportunity to develop deeper spiritual awareness of God's call on your communal life. Such awareness of divine leading opens up fresh potential, even as it asks you to come to terms with some familiar things that may need to change.

In this book, the two of us are inviting you to learn some things that will give you choices about the path God is calling you to imagine. As we extend this invitation, we do not minimize the possibility that in-between times may leave you frustrated. As pastors and teachers who coach congregations throughout the country, we know churches often struggle with transition. When congregations see things shifting, they fear the worst. Moving between point A and point B creates great anxiety among some church members.

Grace for the Journey is written to reframe that anxiety into hope-filled possibility. Congregations often struggle in the midst of transition because they have little preparation or support. We live in a world in which people want to get where they are going, as quickly and painlessly as possible—and churches tend to want the same. However, as we emphasize throughout this book, in-between times are part of the natural rhythm of any congregation.

From time to time, every church will face unexpected transitions that they might not welcome. A changing neighborhood, the unexpected departure of a beloved pastor, a deteriorating building, strong members moving away, or decreasing membership are among the many twists and turns that can lead a congregation toward an unwelcome transition. These experiences usually leave churches feeling uneasy—and for good reason: We do not know what might come next. No wonder so many congregations experience anxiety! Stops and starts in these in-between times tend to throw us off balance—unless we are prepared to encounter them as times of grace-filled possibility. Even transitions that a church greatly desires—such as a new building project or becoming a multicultural congregation—can bring with them a certain amount of uncertainty. Our goal is to help you reframe this in-between time as sacred space when your congregation can rediscover its energy and vision.

Our goal is to help you reframe this in-between time as sacred space when your congregation can rediscover its energy and vision.

Think about the profound spiritual opportunity that transition offers. Biblical stories remind us that the people of God are a people on a journey, often living through in-between times. When they failed to create sacred time and space, our biblical ancestors found it difficult to focus on God's leading, God's providing, and God's calling them to a specific purpose in that specific moment. Just as God calls each believer into a life of love and witness, so too does God call each congregation. That call might express itself a certain way for years; but eventually the circumstances that gave rise to a particular church will change. This community of faith may find itself wondering how to get back to the "good ol' days." But God's invitation to congregations facing these in-between times is more challenging—yet also more faith-filled. God invites congregations to imagine how their own past might influence God's call today and into the future.

*God invites congregations to imagine
how their own past might influence
God's call today and into the future.*

Discovering clarity and strength in the midst of uncertainty is no walk in the park! We want to be clear with you: *Grace for the Journey* is not your typical "how to get it done in five easy steps" book. Nor is it a "road map" that gives you simple directions for moving from point A to point B. Rather, this is a book for congregational discovery and spiritual guidance. We are seeking to help you develop a new perspective, one that can open your church to a deeper understanding of itself and its community.

About Our Approach

Our approach in this book challenges Western individualism by recognizing that human beings create communities that develop their own distinctive character. In this book, we are calling this character "culture." We will say more about what we mean by this term as you continue in this process.

We then weave into this communal framework spiritual exercises that we call "practices."[1] These practices will help your congregation develop an attitude of intentional awareness that will open you more deeply to who you are and whose you are, as a community called by God. This holistic approach offers a revealing analytical framework as well as intentional, congregational spiritual direction. The two of us are convinced that this approach can create benefits that are long-term; it will help guide you wherever your congregation's journey leads.

Churches in transition often get stuck taking the same turns over and over again; they have lost touch with their imagination. The framework you will learn here will stimulate your congregation's imagination. In *Grace for the Journey* we deliberately include a wealth of images, metaphors, and biblical stories, knowing that different images will speak to different readers. All of these images, stories and practices are offered to invoke discovery, imagination, and creativity during your in-between time. We believe this is central to discerning the new potential God offers your church.

Throughout this experience, our intent is to nurture your congregation spiritually. For more than a decade, Beverly has given spiritual direction to transition groups. This experience has taught her the value of the communal quality of spiritual direction. Perhaps this quality is even more important now than ever, since U.S. society is growing more and more individualistic. Even within the church, we tend to think of a congregation as a collection of individuals, rather than as a community with a life and purpose of its own.

Grace for the Journey is about learning how to reframe the experience of transition that is so very common among churches today. We want to teach you to see differently, to deepen your roots, and to become more holistically connected. Through this process, we believe you will begin to detect new spiritual stirrings in your midst. Your community of faith will be able to envision more clearly God's call for its preferred future. We hope, then, that *Grace for the Journey* will be for your congregation a way to create space, so new blessings might abound.

The busyness of our lives as both individuals and as communities of faith pushes us outward, rarely giving us room to stop and listen. In-between times invite churches to create sacred space where we can discover and rediscover God's call. Throughout this book, you will find biblical stories that can serve as reminders of the ways in which God has led and continues to lead faithful (and sometimes not-so-faithful!) followers. You'll learn spiritual practices including reflecting, praying, meditating, and imagining that will enhance the spiritual nurture of your congregation. We say it again: These practices offer sacred space. As you begin to envision divinely inspired possibilities, your church will begin to realize the blessings of leaning into in-between times.

As seminary professors, we often emphasize to our students that leaders must be learners. Through our guidance and coaching in this book, you will learn to pay attention to the culture of your congregation and the community around it. Filling the in-between space of transition simply by doing the same things you've done in the past is neither wise nor useful. Rather, it is more productive to the church's ongoing vitality and faith witness to take time to step back and look at the bigger picture. Transition triggers patterns of energy that, when understood, can be directed as a proactive response to change, rather than as an expression of reactive anxiety. In this book, as we have indicated, those patterns of energy are framed in terms of culture.

In *Grace for the Journey*, we will help your congregation better understand the particular and complex character of the culture that drives it. We will also help you uncover and explore the intricate and subtle ties between theology and culture. You will develop a deeper understanding that will allow your congregation to claim and use the best of your past, and discern God's call afresh as you move into a future. This integrated perspective will help you be prepared for both the new possibilities and the resistance you'll encounter in the midst of any transition, whether now or in the future.

We will explore the transitions experienced by some of our biblical ancestors and see how the people of God have lived into times of change. Like those who have gone before us, today's churches must make choices about how we will respond when we find ourselves in such liminal space. If faith communities are willing to look at who they are and how God's calls them, the choices we make can offer opportunities for transformative and vital witness. *Grace for the Journey* will help your congregation claim transition as a deeply communal and spiritual time, a space of discovery and new life.

> *If faith communities are willing to look at*
> ✓ *who they are and how God's calls them,*
> *the choices we make can offer opportunities*
> *for transformative and vital witness.*

So don't waste the grace of this journey! These are moments of hope and promise. As you journey, the two of us will guide, coach, and act as spiritual midwives. We will help you through your transition and, along the way, you will learn more about your congregation. We invite you, then, to discover and reframe your church's deep energy—for the sake of fresh and authentic witness.

Spiritual Practice

We offer this spiritual exercise to be shared with your congregation in this in-between time. The Scripture below was written for a community in transition. Let these words be a reminder of God's presence and purpose for you as a community of believers.

> But now thus says the LORD,
> who created you, O Jacob,
> who formed you, O Israel:
>
> Do not fear, for I have redeemed you;
> I have called you by name, you are mine.
>
> When you pass through the waters, I will be with you;
> and through the rivers, they shall not overwhelm you;
>
> when you walk through the fire you shall not be burned,
> and the flame shall not consume you.
>
> For I am the LORD your God,
> the Holy One of Israel, your Savior.
>
> I gave Egypt as your ransom . . .
>
> Because you are precious in my sight
> and honored, and I love you.
>   —Isaiah 43:1–4a, adapted

Sit quietly with these words for a bit.

After a few moments, read the text aloud together, with each person replacing the names "Jacob" and "Israel" in the first verse with his or her own name.

Then, after a brief time of silence, read the text together again, this time putting your church's name in place of Jacob/Israel.

After a few minutes of silence, spend some time sharing with one another about what this prophetic word says to you as you journey together through this in-between time.

Carry this text with you. Share it with those who are anxious. And do not fear, because you are beloved and precious in God's sight.

1 Finding Yourself in the In-Between

Now the LORD said to Abram, "Go . . . to the land that I will
show you.
I will make of you a great nation, and I will bless you."
—Genesis 12:1–2

. . . so, Abram went—but he did not go alone!

Although we church folks seldom consider it, we are a people on an amazing journey. Like Abram and so many other biblical ancestors who followed the Spirit's leading to a new place of promise and hope, each of us is traveling a path God has set before us. Like any journey, our path includes twists and turns, high roads and low places we must learn to navigate.

Most people prefer to have a clear idea of where they are going and how they will get there. When planning a trip, some folks turn to maps, while others look to a GPS to guide them. But few of us have the time (or patience!) simply to head out, twisting and turning in circles, never certain where we are or how to get to our next destination. In our instant, want-it-now American culture, we usually seek the quickest and most direct path.

Congregational life is no different. When you decide to join a community, your faith journey takes another turn. You are no longer traveling alone; you have united your individual journey with the journeys of others. Your life will begin to change as you travel with others, even if you assumed your pathway would remain exactly what it was when you climbed on board.

Most of us join churches that seem to have a clear direction, only to discover sooner or later that the roads we travel by faith rarely are smooth. Every congregation faces times in its life together when a blind turn or an unexpected shift takes it down a different road. Suddenly, the church finds itself in an unfamiliar and uncertain place. You try to make sense of your surroundings, to figure out where to go from here. Going back is not an option, but it's not easy deciding where to turn next. This twist in your journey calls your congregation out of its ordinary routine. You have entered an in-between time, a space in which things may no longer feel familiar and comfortable. Naturally, this in-between time brings with it more than a bit of anxiety.

If your community of faith is in the midst of one of those in-between times right now, have no fear. Rather than living in anxiety, this can be for you a time to celebrate—because you have entered a phase that is expectant with grace. This in-between time can become a sacred space for discovering new life-giving possibilities for your congregation.

In-between times can become sacred space.

Called for a Purpose

We began this chapter with a Scripture about Abram's call because we are convinced that, like Abram, every church is called by God—and not just once, but over and over again. Have you ever thought of it that way before? Have you ever considered that your congregation has a calling? Most church folk are aware that clergy are called, and maybe even that each individual believer has a calling. But we don't talk enough about the call that Christ extends to each congregation. Your church is part of the body of Christ: Its members are called together for a distinctive purpose. That purpose—God's preferred future for you as a faith-filled community—is your communal call. It is God's vision for you.

As circumstances shift over the years, God's call on your congregation may change. As that call changes over time—and it will—your church will experience times of transition. The stark realities of these in-between times can be disorienting, yet they are also full of promise. The road ahead will seem winding and the destination uncertain. That is why the call must become your focus, your purpose, your vision.

"Sounds complicated!" you may say. Yes, you are right: responding to God's call is not always easy or clear, and the times when we find ourselves in transition can cause us to shudder. We feel like children in the backseat asking, "Are we there yet?"—we just want to get to the next destination. Yet our journey of faith remains just that—a journey, one that is filled with promising in-between times.

God's call to your congregation varies like a winding road as needs and situations change over the years.

Abrams's Call

As communities of faith called by God, we could consider any number of biblical narratives in thinking about in-between times. Perhaps, however, the most fitting place to begin is with the one whose primary character remains ever linked with the One Big Story. When we listen in on God's call to Abram (Genesis 12ff.), we may be surprised to discover how much is involved in responding to God's call—even before the journey begins.

First of all, Abram needed to be able to listen for God. This is no easy task for people of God today. Listening is not valued in the world in which we live. We hear the noise of voices day and night. In fact, the voices we hear are so much a part of our daily lives that we rarely take time to listen at all. Everybody wants something from us—our children, our parents, our friends, our bosses, our churches. Media voices speak persuasively, selling us whatever they want us to buy or believe. Most of us are bombarded with noisy voices. If we are honest with ourselves, we might become aware that we begin to listen to another's voice only when we need help. In that moment, we hope the voice we hear is trustworthy.

Trust may not seem all that important when your congregation is coasting along, doing what feels comfy and familiar. Not until the road shifts, and the twists and turns cause us to make new choices, do we begin to wonder about which direction is right. Not until we tire of driving on the same familiar roundabout do we think of asking for directions.

Not until we tire of driving on the same familiar
roundabout do we think of asking for directions.

When things are rocking along as usual, it's easy to forget that we are not just another group of people who happen to get together on Sundays. We are a people called by God—and God has a purpose for us. Eugene Peterson, a pastor and respected writer, once said, "The assumption of spirituality is that always God is doing something before I know it. So the task is . . . to become aware of what God is doing so that I can respond to it and participate in it."[1]

Our biblical ancestor Abram was a person of substantial means. He had followed his father, Terah, from Ur to Haran (Gen. 11:31) and had quite a few resources at the time of his call (Gen. 12:5). Abram was no spring chicken, being 75 at the time (Gen. 12:4b). He and his wife, Sarai, had no children (Gen. 11:30), so it is not surprising that his nephew Lot and his family became their travel companions. Throughout those years with his father, moving from their home in Ur to Haran, Abram apparently had learned to listen to God. He had no earthly reason to do so, as his family's wealth was significant for its time. (See also Gen. 13:2.)

Then, a moment came when Abram faced choices. When his father died, Abram could have stayed in Haran, likely inheriting his father's estate. He could have decided to pack up everything and everyone and return to the family home in Ur. The Bible leaves no clues as to what was on Abram's mind as he grieved his father's death. All we know is that he was well-off, aging, married, childless (no direct descendant), and living as a stranger in a strange land.

It becomes clear immediately that Abram paid close attention to the whispers and nudges God sent his way. When God said, "Go," Abram got ready to go. We don't know much about what those preparations looked like. We can see, however, that Abram was a person of faith. We can imagine that he did some sitting and praying and struggling. He must have asked God the big "why" questions over and over again. He probably talked this call over with his wife and friends, who may not have been excited about the possibility of packing up and hitting the road. Surely there were times of disagreement and dismay. Like the chosen ones who were gifted to stand atop that mountain with Jesus centuries later, Abram and his entourage (which included his nephew Lot, and Lot's family) probably just wanted to stay put.

That's what most of us want to do, isn't it? Even if we don't like everything about where we find ourselves, the prospect of pulling up stakes and heading out on an unknown path has little appeal. We don't know much about the conversations Abram had with God and the people around him regarding the call he was experiencing; Scripture doesn't fill us in on those details. But at a certain point, Abram and Sarai chose to listen to God. They trusted this call that was about to lead them on an unknown path. Notice that Abram did not jump up and head out alone. Somehow, he and Sarai convinced a few other people to join them on the journey. Then they took time to gather the animals and supplies they would need to survive and prosper. When all was ready, they finally headed out.

As their journey got going, things did not go so well for Abram and Sarai. Abram appears to have tired of this in-between time. When a famine hit the area and they headed toward Egypt to live, Abram used Sarai as a sort of bait to protect himself from Pharaoh (Gen. 12:10–16). At first, the ruse proved for Abram to be a prosperous one, but it does not seem to be how God intended for things to go. Fortunately, Pharaoh let Abram, Sarai, and their entire party leave Egypt without further incident (Gen. 12:17–20).

Abram still was dealing with transition. He did not live at home anymore, or in the land where his father had moved all of their family. Neither had Abram arrived yet in the place where God had promised him—"the land that I will show you" (Gen. 12:1). To complicate matters, Abram's emergency famine relief plan almost backfired. The call from God that had disrupted his comfortable life was not yet fulfilled.

Abram and his family were still betwixt and between, neither "here" in the familiar nor "there" in their new place, the next chapter, basking in the status of fulfillment. To borrow some terminology from today's world, Abram was living in the in-between condition called "liminality."[2] So, like many of us in a similar situation, Abram was not sure what to do next. Yet in spite of all this uncertainty at the beginning of his transition, Abram did some things right. He listened for the voice of God, because he had faith that God had a purpose for him that was better than he could imagine. Sarai became a conversation partner, as did a few of Abram's friends. All this listening and conversation would have taken time—and then there was all the preparation. Once he was ready, Abram listened some more—and then headed out.

Still, Abram did not go alone on this journey; he brought with him people he could trust. Lot, Sarai, and others who traveled with Abram formed with and for him a community. Hence, in their liminality, that in-between time, they shared a special experience of togetherness known as *communitas.*[3]

> *Communitas emerges when a people in liminality work together toward a common purpose.*

Communitas is a term used to describe a particular kind of community. It emerges within a group of people who all find themselves in the same uncertain, sometimes threatening circumstances. Communitas generates the energy necessary for people to work together toward a common purpose, to overcome common challenges.

Standing Together

During in-between times, we as individuals, and as communities of faith, need to foster communitas. Such moments call for choices that will affect our common life. Together we must decide: Will we keep on doing what we have done in the past, while hoping for improved results? Or will we claim this in-between time of liminality as sacred space graced to us by God?

Even as we write this, we can almost hear your moans and groans:

Okay, but what are we supposed to do in this time of waiting?
We've tried new things before, but they just don't work.
If we wait too long, we will get lost.
We're just plain worn out—don't tell us we have more to do.
If we wait any longer, nothing will get accomplished.
We have to make something happen.
Let's get things back to the way they were.

We understand such moaning and groaning, for we have felt it, too. But remember Isaiah's words: *Fear not!* These words remind you that your congregation is not alone. God will protect you because, together, you are precious and loved and already have been redeemed (Isa. 43:1, 4). As you travel this journey, we invite you to pay close attention to God's presence in your faith community. Throughout this book, we will help you discover ways to be responsive to God as you stand together, ready to be surprised by where the Holy Spirit leads you.

Standing together will be necessary, for you will be tempted at times to stay with things the way they are, or to wish you could return to the way things once were. You will also experience pressure to make something happen *now*! As you begin to learn the importance of understanding who you are as a community of faith, you will discover the importance of standing together. God's preferred future for your congregation, as a sign of hope and possibility in transition, is awaiting you.

We know you feel a certain amount of pressure to move on, to make something happen immediately. After all, Americans are known for being pragmatic and getting things done; this "waiting" and "discovery" stuff is just a waste of time, right? Wrong. The stakes are way too high to simply rush to the next thing. If your community of faith works through a transition effectively, it can be transformative and life-giving. It can lead to meaningful change in thoughts, actions, motivations, and values. However, this will happen only if your community cherishes the grace-filled time of transition as a period of deep discovery.

On this point, consider Abram's story again. Look at the trouble Abram got into when he decided to take matters into his own hands. In order to gain favor with the Pharaoh, Abram made a pawn of his wife, Sarai. He could have lost everything—Sarai, all his possessions, even his own life. Abram had to learn the hard way that moving too quickly to make something happen was not God's desire.

So, as your guides and coaches, we invite you to take your time. Allow this in-between time to matter. Use it as a time of exploration and life-changing discovery in order to take the next step toward God's call for your congregation. And, lest you forget, you are called on this new pathway together!

Abram learned the hard way that moving too quickly was not what God had in mind.

I, Beverly, learned about the importance of journeying together more than a decade ago, as I was preparing the project for my dissertation. After years of sitting with individuals and listening to their faith struggles privately and separately, I facilitated my first Transitions Group.[4] The participants turned out to be twelve women whose situations were as varied as the colors in a bowl of jelly beans. Although most of the women were members of the same congregation and participated in some of the same activities, none of them had any idea about the transitions the others were facing. Every woman's in-between time had been kept private. They were traveling roads with similar twists and turns, but each was traveling alone.

Two of the women were stepmothers, each of whom had been married less than four years; four were recent widows; another was twice widowed and in the process of selling her family-owned business. Two members of our group were in the midst of divorces; another was a recently divorced mother of two. Only one of these women had ever been part of any designated support group.

Through this group experience, each woman's sense of being alone on her journey was transformed. The members of this Transitions Group began to claim the safe space and guidance offered to them, not just by the facilitator but also by fellow pilgrims. All of them were traveling varied pathways and spending long, anxious nights with in-between times. I invited these women to sit together, pray together, listen to one another, speak out of their silent pain and anxiety, explore biblical texts, and journal their prayers. Together, these women discovered and rediscovered ways in which faithful folks can discern God's presence—even in the midst of transition's liminality.

Together, the women of that Transitions Group learned to listen deeply. Confidentiality and trust were crucial issues. A grace margin was established. No one criticized or gave advice to others. Most importantly, they discovered God's faithfulness even in the midst of transition. Even more, I learned from my encounter with those wise Christian women that no meaningful transformation is possible apart from significant relationships with others. Those with whom we share the in-between space can become our companions, and sometimes our guides, as we explore unfamiliar roadways. In our group, we had created a safe, sacred space to explore grace-filled possibilities.

> *No meaningful transition is possible*
> *without communitas.*

In order to move from what feels like chaos to hope and possibility, persons in the midst of transition need what Robert Kegan terms a "holding environment"—a safe space to "be."[5] This experience is harder to achieve than it sounds, yet it is a critical step, nonetheless. In transition, there is a great need to develop an atmosphere where voices may be heard and next steps for the journey may be explored. This becomes a sacred experience, even as those in communitas acknowledge their anxieties together. When we can offer a safe space for communities of faith to share their struggles and anxieties, a promising capacity for thriving in the waiting can be discovered. This kind of communal waiting in the in-between times of transition opens the community to grace-filled possibilities. However, this kind of intentionality takes practice.

People in transition need a "holding environment."

Practice, Practice, Practice

Those of us who spend our lives working with congregations have discovered the value of intentional practices for vital congregations. In *Practicing Our Faith: A Way of Life for a Searching People,* Dorothy Bass and Craig Dykstra remind us that practices address fundamental human needs and conditions through concrete acts. Bass argues that people on a journey need more than a good sermon on hospitality; they need to be beckoned inside, given some supper, and shown where to sleep. That act of faithful hospitality is a deeply spiritual practice in itself.[6] Practices have the power to heal, to shape communities so they might better discern what God is calling them to be and to do. Practices shared in community over time can become sustaining elements of the life of your church's culture. Eventually, as you see some of your ordinary activities as spiritual practices, you will come to perceive how your daily lives are all tangled up with things that God is doing in the world.[7]

Learning to do anything well requires practice. Doctors practice; musicians practice; baseball, basketball, and football players practice. Swimmers swim miles each day as they practice. Ministry, too, is a practice. However, spiritual practices are not something we engage in to try to get better at a particular activity. Rather, these practices cultivate the sacred space necessary to reflect, pray, meditate, and imagine as we grow in our relationships with God and others. They can connect us to one another and to God, helping us touch not only our communal minds, but also our community's spirit. In a world in which people are searching for ways faith might make a difference in their work, play, and relationships, spiritual practices provide avenues for connecting the dots. As you discover and pay attention to ways to practice your faith, you will notice how these practices flow into one another. They help your church focus more intently on listening and responding to God's call on your life together.

In other words, "practicing faith" is not confined to our private behavior. When congregations become deliberate about their practices as a community, they experience new life. This is especially true, Diana Butler Bass argues, when such practices emerge out of a fresh commitment to being open and imaginative. Bass suggests that the "practicing congregation" does not adopt new practices arbitrarily nor does it simply imitate another church it thinks is doing things right. Rather, in the process of seeking a new chapter in its life, the practicing congregation is being intentional about what it does.[8]

Your congregation may already be aware that you are sharing in some meaningful spiritual practices in worship—as you celebrate Holy Communion, or in the sacred moments of Baptism. But you also share spiritual practices in the way your congregation responds to illnesses and death. As you become open to grace-filled possibilities in times of transition, you can discover even more practices. If you let them, they will nourish your common life, quietly preparing you for fresh, vital witness.

One way to lean into an in-between time involves the simple act of intentionally reminding one another of the value of learning how to hold the anxiety as a community. Rather than trying to move forward too quickly—in order to calm the persistent anxiety of transition—you will want to be deliberate about sharing spiritual practices together, as a congregation. Each chapter in *Grace* will help you discover ways to create time for paying close attention to God's whispers and nudges. Spiritual practices provide sacred space to let go of the rush of traffic, work, and family demands. You will be offered a communal focus that can help you set aside for a moment the demands of the dinner that needs preparing and the bills that must be paid. You will center your hearts, minds, and spirits on the presence of the Holy Spirit in your midst, as you live together in the in-between.

Spiritual Practice

Rather than rushing through this in-between time as if you're running through a maze, we invite you to develop a nonanxious presence filled with hope and grace. A nonanxious presence does not deny the challenges and questions raised by your particular transition. Rather, it becomes a way to refocus your energy on God's direction for the pilgrimage you are traveling together.

The ancient spiritual practice of labyrinth prayer can be a way to connect your congregation with God's direction in this in-between time. Medieval Christians built prayer labyrinths to use when they could not get to Jerusalem to worship on high holy days. Today churches of various denominations have created prayer labyrinths not only to strengthen their own prayer life but also as open invitations for others to join them in prayer. These labyrinths include everything from simple pathways lined with stones, to canvas drawings used in indoor settings, to more elaborate stone or paved pathways.

Those who have walked labyrinths often express great relief in knowing they don't have to worry about which way to go or what words to pray. While it may resemble a maze, following the circuit path of a labyrinth does not require you to figure out where to go next. The winding path of the labyrinth leads only to the center. In that center, we stop, focused only on the God who leads. From the center there is only one way out, no decision to be made. Walking the labyrinth is another prayer tool reminding us that God both leads and holds. Our responsibility is to begin the walk, focusing not on how to get out but on how to become more aware of God's presence along the way.

By looking online at www.labyrinthsociety.org/resources, you may be able to locate a nearby prayer labyrinth that you and others in your congregation can visit together. You can "walk" a virtual labyrinth on this website or download and print enlarged copies of the simple finger labyrinth appearing in this book. If you choose to make use of either the virtual labyrinth or a finger labyrinth, you will want to "walk" it several times. If you can arrange to visit a nearby labyrinth for your group or congregation, you will be surprised by the ways your prayer walk changes as you walk together. The steps below invite you to pray with a finger labyrinth:

Begin by centering yourself in silence.

Choose a word or phrase that you will offer as your prayer throughout your labyrinth walk (for example, Come, Spirit; Lead us; Hope; Emmanuel; Center Me).

With eyes closed, repeat the phrase three times, opening yourself to God's Spirit.

When you feel centered, trace the path of the labyrinth with your finger, prayerfully repeating the word or phrase you have chosen.

When you reach the center, rest there. Breathe out your anxiety; breathe in God's possibility.

Continue your prayer as your finger traces the path out of the labyrinth.

Share your thoughts after a time of silence.

2 Naming Your Energy: Discovery and Truth-Telling

> Just after daybreak, Jesus stood on the beach; but the disciples did not know that it was Jesus. Jesus said to them, "Children, you have no fish, have you?" They answered him, "No." He said to them, "Cast the net to the right side of the boat, and you will find some." So they cast it, and now they were not able to haul it in because there were so many fish.
>
> —John 21:4–6

We should not be surprised.

In the midst of grief and anxiety, not to mention a life-changing transition, the disciples headed back to a place that felt normal, natural, familiar, and safe. Little did they know what was in store for them. When all else failed, these guys knew how to fish. They had fished for a living for years. Then one day, this Jesus had called them to follow him, and they dropped their nets and left behind the life they had known.

Now he was gone. Yes, they had seen him twice since his torturous death on that cross, but he was no longer present with them each day, as he had once been. They were filled with the same kinds of thoughts and anguish we all go through when life turns us upside down. "What if?" became the vocabulary of their hearts. Peter was devastated. What if he had not turned his back on Jesus and denied he ever knew him? How could he forgive himself? How could he ever let that memory go? The others knew that they, too, had let their beloved Jesus down. They had behaved as cowards, and life as they'd known and loved it was over. There wasn't much to go back to now. After all, they had left their families, their livelihoods, and their villages. So they returned to what they'd always done: fishing.

For hours, these dejected former members of a religious movement gone bad—and then strangely good again—cast their nets to no avail. There were no fish to be caught, just more frustration—until, unexpectedly, a familiar voice urged them to fish from the boat's other side. For some reason, they listened to that voice and did just what was asked of them. Then, before they knew it, they had caught loads of fish. Their nets filled to the brim, they joined the One whose voice they had trusted, Jesus. Gathered around that small fire on the beach, they shared a meal with him—a meal they would never forget. Once again, nothing was as they thought: It was deeper, richer, and life-changing.

All too often, congregations that find themselves in the in-between time of a transition do exactly what the disciples in John 21 did: They go back to whatever they were doing before the crisis presented itself. This strategy worked out well for the disciples in this story—but only because Jesus was there waiting for them, offering them one more chance to understand who he was and the new thing he was calling them to do. He knew their first inclination would be to go back to their same old ways, doing the same things they'd always done. Jesus had other ideas for them—a purpose that would change the very essence of their lives.

Just like the people in our congregations today, the disciples were part of a faith community that existed within a larger culture. As experienced fishermen, they knew how to function in the fishing-based culture that existed around the Sea of Galilee. They knew what to do, how to do it, and what kinds of techniques might catch different fish. But after leaving their nets behind to follow Jesus, they had become part of the unique community of disciples that arose around their Savior. They had walked with Jesus. They had watched him heal and love those whom others considered unlovable, and now they had experienced great loss. Together they had listened as he taught, and together they had watched him suffer and die. Jesus changed the ways in which their lives would be lived. He changed the ways in which they looked at the community around them. Being with him had affected their particular culture, but now they found themselves living in between.

This thing we call "culture" is the thread, the deep stream, that connects persons within any group, organization, or community. For our purposes in this book, we will focus on the culture created within communities of faith. Every congregation has its own unique culture. It consists of your congregation's own particular set of behaviors, values, and norms, and it emerges as a group of people work together toward a common purpose over a period of time.

Especially in times of transition, looking at your church through a cultural lens will help you get a grasp on what is really going on within you. You will gain a greater understanding of your congregation as the complex, culture-creating, and culture-bearing groups that it is. From there, you can begin to figure out what decisions and actions will serve your purposes more effectively.[1]

In our teaching and work with congregations, we draw attention to three distinctive, yet overlapping ways in which culture functions: in levels, by phases, and across scales of size.[2] For our purposes in this chapter, we will introduce you to the levels of culture by using the metaphor of fishing. You will want to pay close attention to each level, so that you can better appreciate why culture is deeper than the eye can see. It affects everything we do or try to do. Building on this deeper understanding of culture, we can then begin to discover the deep energy of your particular church and become more aware of what feeds and nourishes the life within it. This dimension of discovery will make a difference for your church as it lives through any transition that you will experience, now or in your future.

Without a deeper understanding of its culture, your church may keep throwing out its nets, but you will rarely catch what you want. So, grab your fishing gear, as we begin to learn more about how to uncover your congregation's levels of culture. Let's imagine that we are by the water, eager to haul in a catch.

Deeper than the Eye Can See

Look around the lake, pond, river, or seaside where you like to fish. What do you see there? Are there shells, rocks, or plants nearby? What does the water's edge look like? Are other people fishing around you? If so, what kind of bait and lures are they using? Are they standing on the shore? wading out into the water? sitting in a boat? What does the shoreline or the area around the water look like? Do you have to find your way through bushes or weeds to reach the water? And what about the water itself? It is clear or muddy? Is it flowing, wavy, or calm?

Now consider what you see on the "shoreline" of your church as you arrive on any given Sunday. Try to imagine how you would view it as a first-time visitor. If there is a parking lot, is it full? What kinds of cars are parked there? Are some of the spaces saved for special persons or purposes? Whose names are on those spaces? As you move closer to the building, are there signs that direct you where to go? Do people gather outside or are folks greeted inside the doors? Are folks greeted at all?

What do you see as you wade into the waters of your church? Do regulars dress up or is casual dress typical for your congregation? Do members sit in the same seats each week? Do you have a projection screen or hymnals, a piano or organ, or maybe a full worship band? Is there a choir and, if so, do they wear robes? Do they sing in the front of the church or in a balcony? What does your pastor wear? Do women and children have a prominent role in the worship service? Is there a printed bulletin? What does it include?

In short, what makes your church different from or the same as other churches around you?

All these details, along with everything else that could be seen or observed, make up the first level of your church's culture. It is the level called "artifacts." This level contains the most obvious and observable details of a culture. However, just because this level of culture is easy to see doesn't mean it's always clearly understood. Appearances can be misleading. Artifacts might look the same from one church to the next, but you will soon discover they do not always mean what you might think.[3]

Have you ever visited another church of your denomination expecting the worship there would be the same as—or at least similar to—the worship at your own church? It's common for people to assume that churches of the same "brand name" will be pretty much the same wherever they go. But that's simply not the case. Even in the particular Presbyterian tradition to which we belong, you may walk in to the beat of drums rather than hearing an organ prelude, see a stage set where the communion table "ought" to be, or look for blue hymnals only to discover a projection screen instead. All these artifacts have meaning much deeper than what we can see on the surface; they represent what a congregation sees as important.

What you see may not mean what you think it does.

Peering a little more deeply into the water, you will begin to notice some other things beneath the surface. This second level of culture is called "espoused values," because it is here where we find statements that express the church's ideals. These statements, which can be spoken or written, offer the church's explanation for the artifacts we see on the church's cultural shore. Espoused values are formal positive expressions of a congregation's beliefs about who they are and what is important.

To the members of the particular congregation, espoused values sound good and familiar. "We are a warm and friendly church" is often heard. "Everybody is welcome here" rings loudly in song and in greetings. All the theological statements about "what we believe" are part of a congregation's espoused values. Anything that one can hear spoken aloud as some sort of affirmation can be included in this second level of culture.

Espoused values simply tell us what sounds positive—which, in itself, is not bad. Espoused values are like the reflection we can see in the water itself. The image we glimpse there can be helpful in understanding a congregation. But be careful! What you see and hear in a church's espoused values never provides a complete or fully accurate picture of that congregation or its culture. To get the full picture, as we will soon discover, we need to look even more closely. We need to cast our nets into the deeper waters in order to discover where the real energy rests. This part of the process will be presented in chapter 4, so keep your fishing gear nearby. But first, let's spend some more time considering what we *can* understand from the first two levels of church culture.

*Espoused values simply tell us what sounds
positive—which, in itself, is not bad.*

Back to the Beach

It is no coincidence that the two of us decided to come to the beach to do much of the writing of this book. I (Beverly) have spent more than thirty years enjoying the sunrise and walking along the sugar-white beaches of this part of the Gulf of Mexico. If I focus my morning stroll on the frothy waves, it feels quite familiar. I know it well. That familiarity, and the comfort of knowing what to expect, now draws the two of us back as often as time and resources allow us to break away. Sighting a school of fish looking for breakfast; watching a tiny crab holding tightly as the surf moves—for me, it is all very familiar and quite wonderful.

Now, if we pay closer attention to this familiar beach, George and I begin to notice how things actually are changing moment by moment. On a clear day, if we look for a while, we might glimpse a couple of dolphins dancing in the distance. Yesterday the beach displayed ridges of shells; this morning there are almost none. Sometimes, dark seaweed clogs the shallow water, discouraging the swimmers. A few weeks ago, the beach was filled with umbrellas, chairs, boogie boards, and children of all ages building sand castles and jumping in the waves. Today it's almost empty. This same familiar beach is ever changing, in both big and small ways.

On this recent visit in particular, however, we couldn't help but notice a different scene on this beach. The sun was still shining; the sand remained sugar white; the singers in the television ads were still saying, "Come on down—it's a beautiful day at the beach." But something else was going on. Every morning, a crew of men and women wearing large-brimmed hats, work gloves, and bright green vests came and set up tents all along this beach. An underground oil drilling project many miles away had erupted a few weeks earlier, sending oil hundreds of miles toward the beaches. The green-vested crew was spending its days marching along the water's edge looking for tar balls. Each time we glanced out at the glistening azure waters, we would see these brimmed "soldiers" marching with bags in hand, seeking to capture these tiny balls of unwanted tar beginning to float up from the deep. There were large boats and helicopters too, all working to contain or clean up this unwanted, threatening oil in the waters.

In spite of the danger, the people and the businesses in this relaxed tourist town continue to espouse, "Come on down—it's a beautiful day at the beach." But anyone who was paying close attention was wondering whether the oil would arrive soon and whether this gorgeous beach might never be the same. Nobody wanted to talk about the potential dangers of drilling offshore. Tourists like us never thought about it; the locals didn't discuss it publicly either. We were encouraged to keep our eyes on what was easy to see—the beautiful, the familiar, the comforting. But because we were paying close attention, we worried about what could be lost. The beach culture here could be changing right before our eyes: Its artifacts and espoused values alone did not tell the whole story.

Our beach experience suggests a sobering insight. It reminds us that our congregations typically do not pay attention to the whole story of who they are. However, as you learn to take notice of the culture of your church, you will be more prepared for (and less surprised and confounded by) the things that float up on your shore.

You can begin your fishing expedition by asking a few church members a couple of questions about why they prefer this church to other churches. The answers you hear will be espoused values. The words are true to some extent. But the responses to such direct questions tend to represent what the folks you ask want to believe about themselves and their church. Usually, the answers we get are more about sounding good than helping us understand more deeply what is going on. It is not that folks don't want to tell us the truth; it is much more that what we can discover in the deepest level is not directly on the church's radar.

Pastors often don't realize that churches can run into trouble when they pay attention only to espoused values and artifacts. More often than not, what you see is *not* what you get. Churches say they want pastors to do a certain thing, to take on some pet church project. All too often, the pastor discovers that when she or he does just that, the church's applecart is toppled and chaos begins to take over.

For instance, think about how frequently you hear churches saying they are hungry for new families with children. When children from families outside the church membership come, perhaps to summer vacation church school, or maybe because somebody actually invited these families to attend, all seems wonderful—until you realize the kids who have started attending are nothing like the children you raised. And their families—they don't look or act exactly like the current members, either. Where is that kid's mother on Sunday mornings; why does she just drop her son off and head out? Church members can become frustrated and even angry when things just aren't like they used to be.

What about that young woman who started attending worship a few weeks ago because she heard that "this church has a place for everybody." One Sunday, she reads in the church bulletin that the finance committee will meet on Monday night at 7 p.m. Since she's a certified public accountant, she begins to think this particular committee might be her place in this church; so she comes to that meeting. The table is quiet when she arrives; nobody greets her. When the meeting begins, she listens and finally offers her expertise. Does the committee welcome her input? You can probably imagine this scene. And you're probably not surprised to hear that she never returned to the church again—not even for worship.

Did the members of that finance committee mean to hurt this capable woman's feelings and drive her away? Were they even aware of what transpired? Probably not. In many congregations, however, this is an all-too-common occurrence. As your guides for in-between times, the two of us want you to know that you can learn to anticipate this kind of potential pitfall. Once you begin the process of discovering more about your culture, you learn to appreciate its richness. There is more to what we see on the shore, or even hear spoken aloud, than meets the eye.

As your fishing line begins to drop deeper into the waters, you may sometimes seem to get caught on something. You may not even be aware of what it is at first—maybe a plant, a dead branch, a discarded boot. But try as you might, you just can't seem to get free. Whatever it is seems to be anchored below the water. Your line may get tangled, and the fishing may stop for a while. But don't cut bait! If you want to catch the cultural prize, hang on and hang in there.

It is time now to discover whether what is in the deeper waters feeds the fish or threatens them. We call those things that seem to anchor the pond, lake, or ocean the "submerged beliefs." This is the third level of church culture, the place where your congregation's energy—whether active and productive or dormant, sluggish, and resistant—rests. Even though its particular elements have been "down there" for a while, this third level is rarely noticed or acknowledged, so its various elements are seldom, if ever, spoken aloud. Yet, in order for the fish to thrive in this body of water, their life must be supported and nourished by what is deep below the surface.

The story of Jesus helping his old friends catch fish offers a charming yet telling image of congregations in transition. When things get difficult, we may be tempted, just as the disciples were, to revert back to what we used to do. It is all too easy to be misled by what appears to be floating on the surface. Artifacts and espoused values never tell the whole story. Your church needs to find a way to "cast its net" to another side of the boat.

If you want to understand your church's particular culture, you will learn to engage this process of cultural "fishing." You will want to gather a small, dedicated group of members who are committed to this honest discovery. This group should include longtime members who are "key culture bearers,"[4] as well as some newer, active members too. This fishing expedition takes commitment, hope, and "a sense of urgency."[5]

> *What will happen to our church if we keep on*
> *doing what we have done over and over again?*

The question with which you will want to live is simple: "What will happen to our church if we keep on doing what we have done over and over again?" The time you spend together in this discovery process will affect the road taken during your journey of transition. If you choose to go fishing, there is no better time to begin than now!

Spiritual Practice

As with each of the other spiritual practices offered in this book, one member of your group will need to act as *guide* for this exercise. Have the group sit together in a circle. Turn back to the beginning of this chapter so that the text from John 21:4–6 is in front of you. (If you prefer, you may want to grab a Bible and read the complete story as it appears in John 21:1–13.)

Begin by centering yourselves, taking a few deep breaths.

With eyes closed, sit in silence for a few moments as you prepare to hear again the story.

After a few moments, your *guide* will begin to read the text aloud.

Once the text has been read, sit quietly for a few moments with what you have heard.

After a time of meditation, your *guide* will invite you to reflect on the following questions:

1. As an individual, where do you go when you are confused or upset?
2. What does your congregation do when it is faced with upsetting or confusing news?
3. Using the metaphor offered in this chapter, for what is your congregation fishing?
4. What kinds of "bait" are you using?
5. Where will you go if, like the disciples, you catch nothing?

Sit with these offerings for a few quiet moments.

Now, begin to imagine what your church might experience, if Jesus fills your nets today.

Are you ready?

Share with one another the possibilities you are beginning to imagine. Allow your *guide* to take notes on your conversation for future reference.

When you are ready, take the hand of the one sitting next to you, stand (if you are able), and offer a word or sentence of gratitude to God for the possibilities you are beginning to imagine for your church's future.

3 Cocoons and the Internet: The World at Your Doorstep

I will stand at my watchpost,
   and station myself on the rampart;
I will keep watch to see what he will say to me,
   and what he will answer concerning my complaint.
Then the LORD answered me and said:
Write the vision;
   make it plain on tablets,
   so that a runner may read it.
For there is still a vision for the appointed time.
It speaks of the end, and does not lie
If it seems to tarry, wait for it;
   it will surely come, it will not delay.
                              —Habakkuk 2:1–3

The prophet Habakkuk is frustrated. His people, the people of Judah, are in trouble; they are ignoring God's ways, perverting justice (Hab. 1:3–4). Habakkuk sees this abandonment of their holy tradition as a path leading to destruction and violence. Judah now faces the threat of invasion, from the "dreaded and feared" Chaldeans (1:6–7). The prophet has called and called for God to act—but his cries appear to be of no avail (1:2).

So we find Habakkuk climbing to the top of a watchtower, one of the highest points in the city, to cry out one more time for God's help (2:1). The answer he gets is not the one he probably was looking for: "Wait!" The prophet did not want to do any more waiting. He wanted action, now. But the word from God was clear: Write the vision; make it so easy to read that even a runner passing by could see it. If it seems to take too long, wait for it. It will come at the right time (2:2–3). This was not what Habakkuk wanted to hear! Surely it was *already* the right time. He believed they had waited long enough; besides, what was all this vision stuff about anyway?

In this quick-fix, wireless, technologically crazed American culture, waiting has become a very undesirable option. Today, with the touch of a button, we can not only discover how far away we are from the place we'd like to go, we can also track our own movement by satellite as we travel to that destination. Whenever we need information, the Internet is at our fingertips—at coffee shops, restaurants, and churches, even in the palms of our hands. For people like us, waiting just won't do. (Ironically, being on the cutting edge of the latest technologies may be one of the few things for which people *are* willing to wait. Think about the 600,000 people who lined up to be among the first to get the latest iPhone. For the newest, smartest phone on the market, people actually did wait in line; some even camped out on sidewalks and in parking lots.)

Churches need information, too—and that's especially true of churches in transition. But many churches aren't willing to take time to find out what kind of information can guide them. In order to make your congregation's transition a productive one, you need to know more about who you are as a congregation. You would benefit also from taking time to consider what you can expect when any kind of change knocks on your doors. But that's a lot to ask. People in churches typically don't want to wait—or to change! Throughout this book, the two of us will continue to remind you that in-between time creates space

for possibility and promise. In this liminal space of transition, you have
an opportunity to pay attention to what you might normally overlook.
You do not want to move too quickly: The intentional work you do in a
transition can create positive, long-term effects for your church's ministry for years to come. But it requires an appreciation for the value of
active waiting.

Imagine . . . Your congregation will
learn the value of active waiting.

Three Images of Sacred Waiting

How can you help your congregation appreciate the critical importance
of treating your transition as grace-filled possibility? How will paying
attention to all the cultural aspects of your church and the world around
you make a difference? A genuine awareness of your church, in rela-
tion to both God and neighbor, is absolutely necessary. Otherwise, you
cannot begin to imagine God's preferred future for your community of
faith. Otherwise, you will move too quickly, tempted to "fix the prob-
lem" when you have far too little information.

In your in-between time, this liminal space of transition, you must
learn to pay attention—in new ways—to what you see and hear. You
have already been given some tools for discovering the keys to your congregation's deep energy. In this chapter, you will learn how to look for
clues regarding particular forms of culture that surround your church.
These clues will help your church discover what it previously might not
have had the time or energy to notice. As you pay closer attention to
the cultural streams surrounding your church, you will gain greater
understanding of how they affect, and are affected by, your particular
transition.

We refer in this chapter to the cultural worlds that surround your
church as "streams." As you begin to investigate these streams, you
might find it helpful to think of them in terms of images and metaphors.
Images as diverse as the Internet, a spider's web, the Israelites' wilderness wanderings, and even a cocoon can be illuminating.

Think about it: Transition offers a new opportunity, one that calls a
congregation out of what is familiar and comfortable. We can compare

it to something as natural and complex as a spider weaving its web. Recently, I (Beverly) stepped outside our old farmhouse to find George watching an interestingly hued spider weaving an intricate web, complete with a thick, white, zigzag center. As the spider crawled to the center, the web looked complete and nearly perfect. This web was in front of a window we open and shut every day. One morning a few days later, I accidentally brushed a strand of the web with my hand. That one quick touch was all it took, and the entire web began to change. Although it still looked a lot like the web before I had touched it, my unintentional "interference" had altered it nonetheless.

Transitions affect a church in much the same way. We might think that certain changes affect only a single strand of the congregation. But when even one strand of the congregational web is disrupted, the entire web is in flux. This is what happens to the culture of every congregation when something new appears—whether we acknowledge it or not.

In-between times might be compared also to the biblical story of the exodus. What happened after the Israelites left Egypt? It is clear that their escape from the pharaoh began with a sense of urgency, a great desire to get away from slavery and bondage. It was not long, however, before the Israelites began to doubt if they should have left at all. They seemed to have forgotten the pain and suffering of their life in Egypt. In transitions, the desire to separate from what no longer works creates a sense of urgency, but inevitably doubts will arise in the process. The voice of doubt, like that of Pharaoh, does everything in its power to keep us in bondage to the status quo, the ordered, the known. The world around us pushes and shoves us into taking action—"now!"

> "Just do it, and do it now" is the
> motto of today's society.

If spider webs aren't your thing, and a sojourn like the exodus is beyond your comfort level, what might it look like to reflect on the image of a cocoon? In *When the Heart Waits*, Sue Monk Kidd reminds us of the value of "cocooning."[1] Think about it: A caterpillar gathers everything it needs, crawls into a space that feels safe, latches on to something secure, weaves a shell-like substance around itself, and sits there—waiting.

As the caterpillar waits, it is transformed from a crawler to a beautiful winged butterfly. That transformation cannot happen without a time of waiting—without transition.

An ancient story is told of a man who discovered a creature struggling to get out of some kind of shell. Being a good, kind man, he reached in and tore the shell apart. Tenderly taking the creature into his palm, he looked at it more closely. After careful examination, he realized this creature was almost a butterfly. Its colors were vibrant, but its wings were not yet fully formed. This butterfly-to-be could not fly; it had not been ready to leave the cocoon. Try as he might, this gentle man could not help the lovely creature use its wings. Before his eyes, it fluttered for a while and then died. It had not finished its cocooning, its waiting. Like an infant born before its time, what comes prematurely has little chance of survival.

In liminality, this time of active waiting, you will be tempted to rush forward, to make something happen immediately. Driven by their own fear or control, others may not understand the promise and possibility that arises from sacred waiting. Let us be clear on this point: Active waiting is not about sitting still, tapping your toes, or looking at the clock. Working through transition leads to new life. Those who are content only with keeping on doing what has been done in the past might not be able to imagine fresh alternatives. They may see little use in working with the kinds of models and practices we are teaching you for waiting time. Often others are frightened with new processes, anxious about what might happen to them and their comfortable world.

> *Rather than blessing and encouraging the waiting, some people use power and control to hold the community in its present state of being.*

Don't allow anxiety to distract your church or pressure you to move hastily. You will want to discuss and prepare carefully, inviting certain key folks to participate. Together on this journey, you will be putting your collective finger on various elements of the world around you. These external features affect your congregation more than you may realize; giving them names will help you keep track of their influence.

Getting into the Flow: Cultural Streams

We have mentioned already that culture is made of many different streams. These streams are like creeks and rivers, in that they flow in, around, and through the pond that makes up your church's ministry setting. Cultural streams come in various sizes, from the tiny trickles inside your church, to the larger creeks in your neighborhood or town, all the way up to the wide rivers of American society. We call this phenomenon "cultural confluence."[2]

Your discovery team might decide to begin its process by examining the broadest of these cultural streams, the "macroculture." Think about the value that U.S. society places on independence, "my rights," individualism, democracy, being number one, even baseball and apple pie—not to mention something called "economic opportunity." These examples all point to the presence of a large-scale culture that exists to one degree or another across the United States. Macroculture is that aspect of American life with which everyone in the country must deal, whether they know it or not, understand it or not, like it or not. Many of these macrocultural artifacts and espoused values flow right into the culture of your congregation, shaping you in ways you may not even realize.

What might it mean, for instance, if your church is in an area where local businesses can no longer survive because of a factory closing? What would it mean if your church were located in an area of offshore drilling, where fishing or tourism was a primary way of making a living? What happens to the church when members who have taught school for years find their salaries cut, their benefits reduced, and their job threatened due to budget cuts? What happens to your congregation if many members can no longer find employment in your town? Each of these scenarios is related directly to macroculture. Sometimes changes from this large-scale stream race like a tsunami through your church, reshaping its reality. Active waiting allows time for you to identify these external elements and to consider together how they affect your church's ministry.

However, the macroculture is not the only stream that lives and moves outside your congregation. Between the macroculture and the local culture immediately surrounding your church location exists a scale of cultures that are in between large and small. We call these "mesocultures," from the Greek word *meso*, or "middle." Out of these streams flow distinct cultural presences from a variety of sources. For instance, the various regions of the United States have developed certain cultural characteristics that distinguish them from one another. Our country's many ethnic groups maintain treasured traditions stemming from their nations of origin. The cultural world of old family wealth is very different from that of families and communities who are "just getting by." Generational differences between groups of Americans create distinctive streams at this middle-level of culture. The baby boomers who came of age in the 1960s questioned the practices and values of their parents' "silent" generation. Now, our society is increasingly shaped by the children of boomers, a generation that has grown up in another kind of world—post-civil rights movement, post-Cold War, less idealistic, awash in nanotechnological savvy, and perceiving life through the Internet instead of the morning newspaper.

No congregation can thrive in ministry and witness without paying attention to mesocultural streams. They affect (often very subtly) the ways in which your congregation understands similarities and differences among those who are part of your community. The specific presence and configuration of these streams in your local community will change over time. If your church is to be both hospitable and responsive to change, it will need to keep all sorts of mesoculture on its radar.

In your in-between time, you will want to use your active waiting process to imagine how any particular stream of culture is either flowing through, or being log-jammed by, the culture of your church. Here are a couple of extended examples to help you see how crucial your attentiveness to these streams will be for your church's vitality.

As a woman of the South, I (Beverly) know what food means to the culture of a Southern church: Food is caring. If a family experiences sickness or death, they can expect an onslaught of casseroles delivered to their door. If you are a new pastor in the South and nobody brings you a pie or a cake, watch out! Of course, the food choices vary from region to region. Folks coming into Southern churches from other areas of the country might be dismayed to see tables filled with greasy fried chicken, gravy-laden creamed potatoes, and loads of carbohydrate-filled casseroles and tempting sweets. George always grins when he's asked if he wants his tea "sweet or unsweet"; his response is a dead giveaway that he is "not from around these parts!" Southerners can always tell a *Yankee* when they make faces at our ordering of grits, or begin to pour sugar or milk on them—yuk! George grimaced the first time he saw fried green tomatoes. Imagine that!

Let us also think a little more about the effects of the generational stream on your church.[3] You have probably noticed that older adults in your congregation tend to prefer more traditional worship, while teenagers and young adults outside your doors are often looking for something very different. For these younger generations, music that is faster, sometimes dissonant, with guitars and percussion, feels more like their world. Unless these differences are uncovered and discussed, they can logjam the many streams flowing into and around your church. You then risk dealing more with conflict than possibility, for years to come.

A congregation may become dismayed when its new pastor comes in using fancy theological words that don't mean much to most of its members. This new pastor may not realize that the culture tends to place more value on stories and real-life examples. Streams of culture that flow out of "orality" share wisdom through proverbs and learn through stories. Communities that are primarily oral in culture don't respond to abstract terminology. At the seminary where we teach, we often encounter students whose home congregations send them to seminary with some trepidation, afraid that those students will lose their voice as they earn their theological degrees. They worry that these young will forget where they have come from and their words will lose their meaning. Yet those same congregations have much to offer if their pastors can learn to honor the oral culture. Stories and proverbs give real life to technical terms.[4]

Paying attention to these various streams of culture and discussing them together will help your congregation understand why some folks respond in ways that don't seem to match your expectations. An "oral culture" congregation might better understand the need for active waiting if it is expressed through the metaphor of planting and harvesting. Rather than abstract conversations about the need for new "vision," such churches do better with down-to-earth language—something like, "We need to take time to find out just what God wants us to do to help our neighbors."

Neighborhood Watch

There is a third primary scale to cultural confluence. It is the one that is most easily recognized by those of you who are most deeply connected to your church. We call it the "micro" scale. *Micro* means "small"—but don't let the name fool you. Although smaller in size, it is crucial to the life of your church. All the people and things in the community where your church is located are part of this microstream. This cultural stream includes everything in the neighborhood itself—all the grocery stores, schools, libraries, and churches—as well as all the people involved with them. Did you ever imagine that all those people and institutions would have an influence on your church's particular culture?

What is the neighborhood like around your church? Do most of your members live there or do they commute? Who are the people who live closest to your church? Are they older or younger than folks in your church? Do they look like your members?

As you begin to think more about the microstream of culture that flows around (and into) your church, you will also want to be aware of what is missing and different. It is critical that you take the time in your active waiting to explore this particular stream of culture carefully. So, gather the troops and get ready to take a pilgrimage around and through your church's neighborhood. Walk the streets. Be silent, taking notes on what you see, who you see (or don't see), and how this makes you feel. Look closely at both big and little things. Are the streets well maintained or not? Look at the homes and buildings. What is their condition? Do you see "for sale" or "for rent" signs? Are children running around; is it noisy or quiet? Do people wave at you or ignore you? Is your church's neighborhood different than when your church was first built?

Remember to stay quiet as you walk. Look, listen, and observe the artifacts that surround your church, and make notes about what you see and hear as well as your feelings. What is missing? Can you imagine your neighbors as part of your congregation? What qualities and features of your church might appeal to them? Have you ever asked them to worship with you? You might be surprised at how this outing affects you. This microstream deeply influences the culture of your congregation.

After an hour or so, come together again as a group. When you re-gather, keep your silence at first. Begin your time together by offering to

God in silent prayer what you have seen and felt. Then begin to share your observations and feelings about this neighborhood walk. Explore your discoveries, making sure to have someone record the findings in writing. Invite each participant to share something that surprised, confused, disappointed, or touched them. As you conclude listing your discoveries, take a few more moments of silence.

Next, begin brainstorming ideas about how your congregation might respond to what you have seen. You might begin with questions like these:

- What are some ways God wants us to relate to our neighbors?
- How can we be more involved in our own community?
- If our community is changing, how might we need to change, in order to build meaningful relationships?

This exercise will help you begin to see why intentional, active waiting can make such a difference in your in-between time. You might discover that you are becoming aware, in fresh ways, of how the streams of culture all around you affect your congregation.

After this discussion, we encourage you to put your shoes back on and take another similar outing. This time, have the same group of church folks walk carefully and silently around and through your own church building and grounds. Keep quiet; make careful notes. Again, here are a few questions to help you begin to think together:

- What do people see when they drive by our church?
- What do our classrooms reflect about the value we place on teaching and learning?
- How do our building(s) and grounds appear?
- What spaces have we created for children?
- What does our signage say to passersby and potential visitors?

As you regroup again, sit quietly with your findings and feelings before you begin to share them. Use your active waiting time together to form your own questions about what you have observed regarding your church.

You will be amazed by what can happen as your congregation allows itself to live into the waiting of the in-between time. Imagine what you might discover, as you live into this waiting—rather than rushing to fix, take care of, or move on to whatever seems easiest to do next.

Making Time for Transformation

Earlier in this chapter, we shared images to help you think creatively about the importance of active waiting during transition. A popular children's book makes this point in its own way. In *Hope for the Flowers*,[5] we meet a couple of caterpillars, Stripe and Yellow. Early in the story, Stripe and Yellow enjoy doing everything together. Through all of their adventures, they laughed and played and learned how to love. One day, they decided to join other caterpillars who were climbing high on a pile in order to see what was at the top. As the climbing continued, Yellow dropped off; she did not like the way the others were treating each other. But Stripe kept on climbing.

Separated from her longtime friend and left to struggle alone, Yellow comes upon another caterpillar who is spinning a cocoon. When he explains what he is doing, Yellow is afraid the caterpillar is talking about dying. In his reply to her fear, the spinning caterpillar tells Yellow: "Life is changed, not taken away."[6]

Still unsure, Yellow asks what she would have to do to experience this same change. Her new friend replies: "I'm making a cocoon. It looks like I'm hiding, . . . but a cocoon is no escape. It's an in-between house where change takes place. . . . During the change, it will seem . . . that nothing is happening—but the butterfly is already becoming. It just takes time."[7]

Yellow is still afraid—not only afraid for herself, but also afraid she will never see Stripe again. Finally, she takes the risk and spins her own cocoon; now, her waiting begins. One day, after much waiting, she emerges from the cocoon and unfolds her beautiful wings. Suddenly, Yellow understands: A cocoon is no escape; it just takes time to be ready to emerge.

A cocoon is no escape;
it just takes time to be ready to emerge.

Throughout this chapter, we have encouraged you to live into the "waiting" of your in-between time. Images of the exodus, spider webs, the Internet, and cocoons remind us that getting ready to move into a new way of understanding takes time. Your church has its own culture, and in order to make this transition transformative, you will need to understand that culture in new ways.

Yes, culture is complex—because the communities that people create are complex. Once you learn how to pay close attention, you will be able to use this discovery process for every transition you encounter. So, get ready to dig even deeper. You are preparing to discover the sources of energy to be found at the deepest level of your church's culture.

Spiritual Practice

This practice is designed to be used after the two "walkarounds" described earlier in this chapter. Once you and your group have completed these walks, gather once again.

As you continue in a spirit of reflection, sit together quietly in a circle. Allow yourselves a few moments of quiet, so that you can be fully present during this time. Then open your hearts and minds as your *guide* for the practice slowly reads the story of Jesus and the Samaritan woman. Relax and let the text live into you as you listen to the following:

> A Samaritan woman came to draw water, and Jesus said to her, "Give me a drink." (His disciples had gone to the city to buy food.) The Samaritan woman said to him, "How is it that you, a Jew, ask a drink of me, a woman of Samaria?" (Jews do not share things in common with Samaritans.) Jesus answered her, "If you knew the gift of God, and who it is that is saying to you, 'Give me a drink,' you would have asked him, and he would have given you living water. The woman said to him, "Sir, you have no bucket and the well is deep. Where do you get that living water? Are you greater than our ancestor Jacob, who gave us the well, and with his sons and his flocks drank from it?" Jesus said to her, "Everyone who drinks of this water will be thirsty again, but those who drink of the water that I will give them will never be thirsty. The water that I will give will become in them a spring of water gushing up to eternal life." The woman said to him, "Sir, give me this water, so that I may ever be thirsty or have to keep coming here to draw water."
>
> —John 4:7–15

After the text is read aloud, allow time for reflection before considering the questions below. Following a period of silence, the *guide* will pose each question, give time for reflection, invite responses, then move to the next question:

1. As you think about this story, with which of the following persons could you most readily identify?

The Samaritan woman?
The disciples?
The villagers peering out their doors and windows?
Jesus?

2. Reflect on what you might have "seen," heard, experienced, or felt
   if you had been present that day.
3. As you continue to reflect on this story, imagine how your congregation might respond to this woman today.
4. How do your responses reflect what you are learning about your
   church's culture?
5. How are your responses now different from what they might have
   been before you began reading *Grace for the Journey* together?

As your time together comes to a close, stand (if you are able) and
take one another's hands as you trust God to hear the words you pray
together:

God of tender mercy,
We admit to you that we are uneasy when strangers come to this
    well of hope.
Your Word reminds us that we all seek the living waters you of-
    fer to us in Christ.
Forgive us when we hold tightly to what we believe belongs to
    us, fearing that there is never enough.
Open our hearts and minds to new possibilities for sharing your
    abundant love as we live into this in-between time together.
We pray as we would live, following the One who offers the
    spring of water gushing up to eternal life, Jesus Christ.
    Amen.

4 Digging Even Deeper: Sources of Congregational Energy

> And the people said to Joshua, "No, we will serve the LORD!"
> Then Joshua said to the people, "You are witnesses against your-
> selves that you have chosen the LORD, to serve him." And they
> said, "We are witnesses." He said, "Then put away the foreign
> gods that are among you, and incline your hearts to the LORD,
> the God of Israel." The people said to Joshua, "The LORD our
> God we will serve, and him we will obey." So Joshua made a
> covenant with the people that day, and made statutes and ordi-
> nances for them at Shechem.
>
> —Joshua 24:21–25

Within the sweep of the Big Story that weaves throughout the Hebrew
Scriptures, we run across moments here and there that help define that
very Story. Amid the dramas of Creation, Fall, Flood, Babel, Abram
and Sarai, Jacob and Esau, rescue from famine, escape from slavery,

wilderness wanderings, conquest, inheritance, judges, prophets, kings, exile, and all the rest—within these many episodes and their layers of richness, we discover a few key pivot points.

One such pivot point for the Scriptures is found in Joshua 24. It represents a memory of a major shift in the holy story of the long-beleaguered community that carries the name of one of its honored ancestors, Jacob—now called "Israel." After generations of ups and downs, scrapes with annihilation, deception from within and without, unlikely heroes, and unexpected turns of events, the twelve tribes had each received portions of land for inheritance. The Promised Land for the People of Promise had been established at last!

It is hard for us to imagine what it must have been like for the Israelites to see that their long-held hope had been fulfilled. Now, they simply wanted to get on with their lives—to forget about all the hardship, the fear, the years of wandering, and live a "normal life." No more uncertainty or anxiety—now it was time to experience stability and abundance.

So why would Joshua seek to spoil the party? In this episode that closes out the book of Joshua, we find the newly-landed former slaves and nomads in a very solemn moment. Joshua does not let them off the hook: He plays hardball with their memory and their loyalty. He does so first by requiring that all the various officers of the nation participate in a religious ceremony (Josh. 24:1—"they presented themselves before God"). Then, according to the text, Joshua addresses the entire nation— "all the people" (v. 2a). He begins by reviewing their Story. Who are they as a people? And how did they end up where they are, in "a land on which you had not labored, and towns that you had not built, . . . eat[ing] the fruit of vineyards and oliveyards that you did not plant?" (v. 13).

The only answer to these questions, of course, is God. The new fortunes of this called people result directly from the initiative of "the LORD, the God of Israel." Israel's very existence, its survival, and now its earthly blessings all are due God's actions on their behalf, over many years and in all kinds of circumstances. As Joshua recites for them a condensed version of the story that spans the first six books of the Bible, it becomes unquestionably clear who should receive the credit for the long-awaited Promise coming true. It is the LORD, and no other.

But the chapter does not end there. For Joshua, simply retelling the story is not enough. It serves a larger purpose—to remind the Israelites of all the reasons that compel their community loyalty. Joshua wastes no words in getting to his point; he moves quickly to the transition, using verbs that are clear and direct: "revere," "serve," "put away" (v. 14). As though he were throwing down a gauntlet, Joshua makes it unmistakably obvious that his people must decide: "choose this day whom you will serve . . ." (v. 15a). The rhythm of Joshua's speech comes to a dramatic conclusion as he declares his own loyalty: "but as for me and my household, we will serve the LORD" (v. 15b).

For Joshua and all the Israelites, this is a moment of high commitment. In the verses that follow, Joshua and the community that he led to this new land exchange words three times—each time concerning the strength of their decision to follow God. It is as though Joshua wants to be sure they know what they are doing. "The people" (a term used seven times in this exchange) affirm each time that they will be loyal to God, that they will accept the responsibility for serving YHWH, the LORD, the same God whose actions over the generations brought them to this place. So solemn was this moment that Joshua marked it by drawing up a covenant and then setting up a large stone in the place where the people worshiped (v. 26). As his final public act before he died, Joshua reminded the people that the stone would be a witness to their decision "this day" to serve God.

Biblical drama of this magnitude catches our attention, does it not? "Choose this day" and "we will serve the LORD" express much of the heart of the Bible's witness. At least for a moment or two, we are moved by the deep devotion expressed by our spiritual ancestors. Our breath catches a bit as we read that the people kept their commitment "all the days of Joshua, and all the days of the elders who outlived Joshua" (v. 31). Surely this is inspiring biblical storytelling. We would hope that it would encourage our own congregations to be so devoted to God.

And yet . . .

As the story of God's people continues in the next biblical book (Judges), we discover that the Israelites found it hard to sustain this devotion in the long run. Indeed, much of what we read in Judges, 1 and 2 Samuel, and 1 and 2 Kings recounts painful communal memories of the people's going back on their promise to Joshua. Over the many decades, the descendants of Joshua's generation found it challenging to uphold the heartfelt commitment that was made years earlier at Shechem. Instead, their former life of fertility gods and Egyptian deities kept calling to them; that world was older, still familiar, and apparently more attractive than this God who refused to be known by an image.

With a story as wondrous as theirs, how could this community—brought into being by the God of all creation—ever turn away? How could it forget all that God had done? This people, our spiritual ancestors, had been in "in-between times" for many years and had seen how God worked amazing things on their behalf. Surely they could hold onto their memories and stories!

The lure of "what used to be" is a strong one, is it not? Leaving the past behind can be challenging, just as surely as fresh, focused energy can be difficult to maintain.

Because the Bible tells such a long story, we today have the benefit of ruminating on the shifting circumstances of our ancestors in faith. As we study their story, we realize that, more than once, they experienced being "in between." When our ancestors were in this condition, they often found it difficult to move ahead by being open to God's leading. Even after moments of dramatic commitment such as the one in Joshua 24, it often seemed easier for the people of God to get anxious, to cling to familiar ways, to resist new possibilities. The story of our ancestors is, in part, a story of how theological and spiritual convictions can get undermined—how even faithful people can get tripped up as they try to pursue good intentions.

Using the Cultural Shovel

In this chapter, we hope to help you develop a deeper understanding of why in-between times present such challenges to churches. It would be easy for us to blame ancient Israel's bumpy fortunes after Joshua 24 on a simple drifting away from faith. Biblical chroniclers who retold many of these stories typically had harsh words for kings and generations whose actions betrayed loyalties other than to YHWH. Yet the realities of their situation—and of ours—are much more complex and nuanced. In-between times present a more intricate set of circumstances than we realize. Many of these intricacies can be seen more clearly when we frame them culturally. In other words, by paying closer attention to the distinctive qualities of our own congregation's culture, we will discover the sources of energy that will determine (albeit obliquely) how we navigate our in-between journeys.

As we have noted in chapters 2 and 3, church culture is much more complicated than we usually realize. Congregational matters that appear at first to be easily manageable can turn out to be bewilderingly convoluted. I (Beverly) once served a congregation for which fresh flower arrangements in the chancel were a valued part of weekly worship. Particular church members contributed money to ensure that identical floral designs graced both the left and right sides of the chancel. Being relatively new to this congregation, I had no idea how important this practice was until the Sunday when only one arrangement was delivered to the church building. I have done plenty of decorating with cut flowers in my day, so my on-the-spot solution was to enlist the help of a church member. We divided the one arrangement into two and put both vases in their usual locations. After finishing the task, we set the vases in place and went on with other Sunday morning preparations.

It never occurred to me that the slight differences between the two arrangements would attract anyone's attention—but they most certainly did so! Two women who take the flowers to shut-ins every Monday told me that they were so distressed by their lack of symmetry that morning that they could not focus on the morning sermon. Another church member called the florist the next day and told him the arrangement had not been up to the standards the church expected. Flustered, the florist called me to find out what had happened to the one vase he had delivered. None of the church members who voiced their dissatisfaction were from the family that had paid for the flowers that week.

In this chapter, we will examine why moments like this—moments filled with such unexpected and unfavorable energy!—occur in our congregations. Responses like these involve more than the personalities and preferences of the persons involved; rather, their behavior plays out on a stage that is deeper and filled with more props and scenery than anyone typically realizes. If a congregation's collective tail feathers can get ruffled this easily over flower arrangements, you can imagine what happens when a congregation faces a transition.

When the Israelites promised, and promised again, that they would serve YHWH, their God, they surely spoke with utmost sincerity. In the language of chapter 2, they expressed an "espoused value," a positive statement representing something of acknowledged importance within the community. The written covenant and the large stone that Joshua set in place were "artifacts" deliberately associated with the peoples' expression of this espoused value. However, we must learn to realize—in both biblical times and in our own congregations—that cultural realities involve more than artifacts and espoused values. They also involve what we refer to as "submerged beliefs." Whether we are aware of them or not, submerged beliefs are the source of the energy that drives our congregations. This point cannot be overemphasized.

In this chapter, then, we turn our attention, to learning about submerged beliefs—what they are, where they come from, why they are so potent, and what happens to them in "in-between times." Submerged beliefs, despite being "hidden" in any organization, are what define the sources of its deepest energy. So, for a church that acknowledges its "in-between" status, this aspect of our cultural comprehension should not be ignored. In our years as pastors, seminary teachers, and church coaches, we have become all too aware of the power of submerged beliefs. *If your congregation does not find a way to manage submerged beliefs, they will control your church in ways that are not easily constructive.* In-between times are critical "kairos" moments in which discovery of your submerged beliefs becomes one major key to grace for your journey.

> ✓ *Submerged beliefs are the sources of a*
> *church's deep energy.*

We spoke in an earlier chapter about our recent visit to the beautiful beaches of the Florida panhandle. During that visit we became aware of how the power of a congregation's submerged beliefs is something like that of the surf's undertow. Tides represent the ebb and flow of the water as it washes up on the sand and then retreats, as another wave moves toward the dry sand right behind the previous wave. It is much easier to recognize the power of a wave as it crashes on the sand than of the undertow that follows it.

Undertow is low and deceptive; it can catch you off guard if you do not pay attention to it! Undertow can make you lose your balance. This almost invisible force is responsible for numerous beach deaths every year. Depending on the conditions, undertow can surprise any swimmer with its sudden and strong energy pulling back. This natural reality of an ocean or large lake cannot be ignored. At the same time, however, it is the undertow that leaves the sea's treasures along the sand—the shells, the agates, the starfish, the kelp, and so on. Thus, undertow is not bad, but it does have to be accounted for, if you are going to enjoy playing in the surf.

Culture is like the surf: If you do not recognize the power of submerged beliefs, their undertow can seem menacing and upsetting.

Understanding Submerged Beliefs

Because we want you to be fully equipped for your congregation's journey, we will seek to be as clear as possible about submerged beliefs and the essential role they play in church culture. In the bulleted statements on the next few pages, you will find a number of interrelated statements about submerged beliefs, with elaboration following each.

- Submerged beliefs make your church's culture what it is. Regardless of the appearance of the church's artifacts or the sound of its espoused values, submerged beliefs define a congregation's cultural energy.

In our denomination, pastors seeking a church call are required to follow a particular format when writing their resumes. In a similar way, churches seeking a pastor follow a specific format in presenting information about the church for pastoral candidates. Prospective pastors provide data about educational background and work experience, responses to pastoral skills rankings, and short answers to questions about theology and ministry. The churches provide statistics about membership, worship attendance, church school, facilities, and budget, as well as statements about mission, theological issues facing the church, and rankings of the skills they seek in a pastor.

What do these respective documents reveal about the pastoral candidate and the seeking congregation? In the language we are using here, these materials identify a lot of artifacts and some espoused values of both the candidate and the congregation. Years ago, the two of us used to think this type of information was adequate for a search process. If the pastor and congregation looked good together on paper, we felt the only question remaining was "fit" and the leading of the Holy Spirit. The church had to ask itself: *Do we "like" him or her, and do we sense the Spirit's urging?* The potential pastor had to consider the same basic questions about the congregation. If the answer to all these questions was "yes," it was a match made in heaven!

Now we look at the search process differently. We have become very aware: The elements that hold the strongest energy for congregation are rarely stated on paper or addressed in an interview process. It is true that artifacts often provide clues that can be helpful in discerning whether the submerged beliefs of a congregation are compatible with those of a potential pastor. Use of the same theological language (espoused values) is, in some ways, even more indicative of some level of compatibility between a congregation and a candidate. Yet these two levels—artifacts and espoused values—cannot tell the whole story. The more perplexing matter is discerning whether the visible artifacts and espoused values hold any relationship to particular submerged beliefs. However, since these deeper beliefs remain hidden, it is almost impossible to determine this.

Therefore, do not be misled by privileged artifacts or favorite espoused values! They are preferred because of their mysterious ties to one or more unspoken, submerged beliefs.

- Submerged beliefs are those deeply held convictions that are rarely spoken aloud yet represent various "principles" that your church takes for granted as right and true.

The discussion about pastoral search processes also helps us to understand why submerged beliefs hold such surprising power. Especially in religious organizations, statements of a theological or spiritual nature are highly regarded. Members of these organizations, therefore, are easily misled about which of their community's characteristics are most foundational. What can be readily stated aloud, as articulate and inspiring as it might be, is not capable of giving voice to premises and assumptions that exist outside of common consciousness. Instead, the two of us are arguing that it is within the nature of human communities—even religious ones—to assume that some of their most deeply held convictions are simply "the way it is," without even realizing it. This lack of awareness is normal, and it helps to explain why differences of opinion about certain artifacts or espoused values can be so potentially explosive.

- Submerged beliefs develop in every organization without conscious or deliberate attention, which is why they require such intentional effort to identify.

People do not sit around and "invent" their own submerged beliefs! Culture does not get created that way. Rather, the process of culture creation for any new community is subtle, intuitive, and indirect—but inevitable and powerful nonetheless. We are not used to thinking about them, so submerged beliefs can seem elusive until we get the hang of what it takes to figure out—for our faith communities—what these beliefs are.

- Unless they are deliberately sought out, submerged beliefs almost always remain outside the awareness of those who are part of your congregation.

People who have been members of your congregation for a long time cannot recite a list of its submerged beliefs! Even though these members know "in their bones" what these deeply held assumptions are, they will find it almost impossible to identify them without appropriate assistance. This is because of the way in which culture operates. The artifacts and espoused values of any organization act almost as veils or prisms, slanting light in ways that prevent a clear look at what lies beneath common awareness. Ironically, the people who are more likely to be aware that there is "something below the surface"—something that does not necessarily square up with what is more obvious—are the newer members. They have not yet become accustomed to the cultural rhythm of the ways in which specific artifacts, espoused values, and deep beliefs are related to one another. For this reason, newer members of your congregation often can be useful as cultural observers: They can see more quickly and clearly the relationships between cultural levels that longtime members have come to take for granted.

- ✓ Even in religious organizations, submerged beliefs have nothing directly to do with religion or faith—although they exist within a religious context.

It shocks many of the students in our seminary classes to learn that a congregation's deepest convictions are not religious in nature. Religion tends to generate strong commitments, which typically are identified with the most primal of cosmic and human elements. Persons who are deeply involved with a particular style or tradition of faith characteristically find it difficult to distinguish the impulses of their convictions from the specific forms with which they are most comfortable. In short, religion gets so tied up with culture that the two can get confused.

We will see later in the chapter some common sources and categories of submerged beliefs. Once you get a feel for these categories, it will be easier for you to begin identifying your own congregation's deep assumptions. As you do, it becomes even clearer what kinds of challenges and opportunities your congregation faces during its in-between time.

- ✓ The strongest submerged beliefs tend to be created in a church's formative years, and they are remarkably persistent over time.

Like any other organization, churches are heavily influenced by the experiences of their earliest years, the decisions that were made, and their responses to situations that came up. From an organizational standpoint, these experiences, decisions, and responses tend to arise from a number of relatively predictable issues that cover both internal and external factors.[1] Because culture is so durable, the founding beliefs and assumptions will outlast their creators, usually by many generations. In other words, members who join your church many years after its founding are enculturated into a particular, idiosyncratic world of deep energy that is subtle, strong, and durable.

- Submerged beliefs come about as the result of how the members of the church (especially those from the earliest years) perceive its achievements in light of its efforts.

During the earliest phase of a church's life, submerged beliefs come into existence. They are a consequence of how the congregation construes the effectiveness of its efforts. The founding members will have an inordinate influence in giving rise to many of these unquestioned premises; culture creation is not a democratic process. How the founding pastor and/or key members deal with issues has a direct effect on what submerged beliefs develop. The "cultural baggage" that these persons bring with them will inform the process of decisions, actions, and perceptions.

- Many submerged beliefs originated outside your congregation and entered it through the presence and influence of strategic founding members.

This point has been mentioned previously, but it needs further elaboration. New organizations are heavily affected by the cultural worlds that founders bring from prior life experience. Such cultural worlds receive their particular character from a variety of sources, including where one was raised, racial and ethnic background, gender, socioeconomic location, and age cohort.[2] Whatever deeply held premises "took hold" in the persons who founded your church will have been put to the test in its early years. This is not surprising, since we are hardly likely to be aware of our own cultural "stews"—the deep energy of culture does not usually operate at the conscious level.

- Submerged beliefs are not necessarily good or bad; however, they do reflect the unconscious conclusions drawn from the congregation's earlier experiences and perceptions.

This point extends an idea we have been discussing already. In one sense, the cluster of submerged beliefs that comprises your church's deepest source of energy should be understood as neutral, in the sense that "they are what they are." They represent the aggregated knowledge gained from its life together. In other words, they stand for what "worked" at some point. This makes quick judgments about the positive or negative value of these beliefs not nearly as helpful as one might suppose. As we will see, the real question is whether the conditions that gave rise to any particular belief still warrant maintenance of that belief.

- Submerged beliefs tend to get disrupted when the congregation's familiar and comfortable conditions change, for whatever reason.

It is important to realize—as has been suggested—that all your church's deepest convictions have a specific context in the congregation's history. Events, situations, experiences, decisions, perceptions all can be analyzed within their particular locations—time, geography, social and economic conditions, etc.—as well as within the church's own very idiosyncratic life. As long as the circumstances that supported your church in its earlier phase of life persist, its submerged beliefs also will continue to serve it effectively. However, the twenty-first-century world is one of rapid and expansive change (digital technology alone illustrates this rapidity and expansiveness). Even in the most traditionally stable of environments, it is difficult to find a community that is "exactly the same" as it was fifty years ago—or even thirty years ago.[3]

Resistance to change is common, both among individuals and within communities. Beyond this general point, recognition of the importance of submerged beliefs deepens our insight. It can help us see that the artifacts that usually get identified as resistant to change do not, in fact, stand on their own. Rather, they always—we repeat, *always*—are tied in some way to particular (unconscious) submerged beliefs. These beliefs contain the community's energy—which is why, when threatened, the result is disruption, anxiety, and resistance.

- Submerged beliefs do not change quickly or easily; changing them requires time and a lot of deliberately focused determination. This work is difficult—but possible and, occasionally, necessary.

Your church's deeply held premises are powerful in part because they have become embedded in your culture over time. In itself, there is nothing innately "wrong" with submerged beliefs being so resilient. If culture could change easily, human life would be even less stable than it already is these days! Culture acts as a group's conserving mechanism, a function that can be both useful and problematic—depending on the circumstances.

Since this book seeks to provide your church with a model for traversing journeys of transition, it is highly relevant to speak about the relationship between change and submerged beliefs. For instance, the central reason that changes in a congregation's worship are often so hotly contested must be found in the deep realm of the church's submerged beliefs. What these beliefs sound like will depend on the specific congregation; there is no one "reason" for such congregational tensions. At the same time, however, a congregation can use awareness of its cultural depths as a tool for being proactive and positive about how it handles its in-between times.

- Learning to pinpoint your congregation's submerged beliefs takes practice, time, revision, and patience.

In the twenty-first century, we have become increasingly accustomed to getting all sorts of things done quickly. Cultural awareness, however, will not bow to speed or expedience. Because the theory that identifies submerged beliefs as the key to culture is still not widely used, it will take your church more time than you might expect to learn to think culturally. This kind of process is not something any of us is used to doing! If you or your church gets too impatient, you will lose the pivotal opportunity that you need to make the most of being in between.

Rummaging through the Surf

Grace for your journey involves giving your congregation the freedom not to know it all—of taking time, of talking and listening and probing, of wondering and guessing, of writing down and revising. What would it have been like for the Israelites in Joshua 24 if, having recently arrived in the Promised Land, they had understood the challenges of espousing "new" values in the face of the longstanding, deep premises about security that were expressed in their earlier religious practices? It is as though they had made idols, not merely of the fertility gods and goddesses, but of the submerged beliefs that upheld those practices. They needed time and a new set of experiences, incidents, and events that would affirm the story Joshua told them. As new artifacts these new experiences would have led the Israelites to acknowledge within community that their ancient story was "true," that it was what defined and guided them as a people. Instead, their story became dogged with many episodes of "lapsing" into idol worship.

Those things in our church's life that are familiar also can act as undertow. They are tied, almost inexplicably, to the deeper currents of culture, invisible forces that we only barely recognize. As we mentioned above, undertow is a natural part of any large beach—but it can be dangerous if we ignore the way it works. When I (George) was a child of about eight, my family went with some other church families for a day along the Oregon coast. Oregon's beaches are rarely warm enough for long days in bathing suits, but the sand, tides, and volcanic rock formations provide plenty of opportunities to explore and enjoy. On this day, the parents were sitting in the sand back from the water while a bunch of us kids were running around in the surf. Even in the summer, Oregon beach water is brisk, so I chose not to get very wet. Instead of splashing around, I had found a spot where tide and sand were meeting each other rather quietly, and I had settled in to looking for agates.

I had not been crouched over this little piece of the beach long before I somewhat absently became aware of someone running past me into the surf. After a few more moments, my peripheral vision picked up movement again, this time coming away from the water. When I looked up, I saw one of the other dads carrying my twin brother in his arms. Mr. Coleman's sweatshirt and shorts were dripping wet as he held my brother, and it took me a few moments to figure out what had happened. He must have seen my brother fall down in the water and, without hesitating, ran from his beach chair to rescue him.

What had caused my brother to lose his balance in the water? We know the answer: undertow. My brothers and I had not played in the surf enough to gain the feel of its ebb and flow. Waves break onto the sand, and then the water recedes—and when it pulls back, it pulls! If my brother had been seriously injured by this one scary episode with undertow, I wonder how I would have been affected. Would I have blamed myself for not paying attention? After all, I had been the closest person to him at the time. Yet, I had not noticed his sudden precarious situation: I had been looking down at the sand and surf in front of me. Even if I had seen my brother and had run to help him, my ignorance about undertow probably would have left me in the same scary situation.

We trust that this point is clear to you by now! Undertow is a fitting image for the realities facing churches that try to be intentional during in-between times. Sometimes, these realities are of the "hard-knock" kind. If churches do not learn to pay attention to its deep energy, it can and will "pull back" and knock the congregation off its feet. Now as an adult, when I go to the beach, I pay attention to the tide and how it is pulling. I have learned from experience that, if I leave my feet in one spot too long, the undertow begins to bury them in the sand—and the next strong wave could knock me down. If I am looking only at the surface of the water, I start to get dizzy in a few seconds—the undertow will throw me off.

The "Sound" of Submerged Beliefs

So far in this chapter, we have talked about submerged beliefs in general terms—defining them, situating them in your congregation's culture, explaining their nature and influence, and suggesting how this deep energy affects your in-between world. What we have not discussed yet in any detail is the character of these deeply held convictions. What do they sound like? Of what life themes do they speak? If they do not sound like espoused values (a common error, especially when you first begin this kind of discovery), what does it take to uncover them?

A considerable amount of cross-cultural anthropological research suggests that these deeply held community premises are distinguishable into several types.[4] For our purposes in this book, we do not need to discuss all of the categories—which include things like reality, truth, time, space, human nature, human relationships, and human activity. But as a way of helping you get oriented to your own congregational self-discovery of submerged beliefs, let us look at a few examples. We think you will find these "samples" easy enough to recognize, and they will help steer you in the right direction. We have implied already that

certain kinds of submerged beliefs are shared among many congregations, because of their sources in streams of culture found broadly in our
society. The ability to recognize this more common stream of unspoken
assumptions will help you become even more discerning of those that
have developed out of your congregation's own specific experience.

TIME

Both of us grew up in Protestant congregations that, despite certain obvious differences, held some basic submerged beliefs in common. One
of these concerns time. For instance, when you ask the members of most
Eurocentric (white) congregations what time worship begins, regardless
of whether the church is Methodist, Baptist, Presbyterian, Episcopalian,
or some other denomination, you probably will get the same answer:
"11:00 sharp." If you ask when the worship service is expected to end,
the reply almost undoubtedly will be "12 noon." Both of us have heard
many stories over the years about hapless new pastors who tried to
lengthen the worship service and met surprising resistance. What is going on here?

By contrast, Sunday worship times for African American churches
are noticeably different. Even if worship is advertised as beginning at
11:00 a.m., it usually gets going at about fifteen minutes after the hour.
As for the length of the service, two hours or more is typical—but the
ending time varies. The clock is not being watched. Rather, the service
begins when everything and everyone is ready; the service ends when
everything is done.

If we want to appreciate the nature of these deeply held beliefs about
time, it is important to realize a few things. First, this difference is not
about race, but about culture. There is nothing inherent about skin color
that dictates an ethnic group's perspective on time. Second, the difference is not religious in nature. Both traditions here are Christian, and
we would be hard-pressed to find—in the Bible or in any other widely
accepted source of authority—specific requirements about the use of
time in worship. Third, there is no ultimate court of appeal for deter-
mining that one view on time is right and others are wrong. As we have
discussed previously, what is important for gaining cultural awareness
is accepting the realities that we encounter. Finally, preference is not the

same as judgment. Just because your group holds a particular unquestioned premise about time does not mean other premises are inferior. We can learn how to understand our own preferences better without presuming to think less of others for theirs.

All these points will be helpful to your church in its journey. When your church is in an in-between stage, it is quite helpful to learn how to suspend judgment about what you discover—especially about yourselves.

With these reminders before us, what do these two contrasting sets of artifacts about typical white and black worship services imply about time? Research helps us realize that different human communities make different assumptions about time.[5] It is true that one perspective, the "monochronic" view, has come to dominate Western societies over the last few centuries. Communities who hold to the monochronic view of time assume that it is quantifiable: Time can be divided into segments, and sequences from first to next to last are important. As a result, time also can be "wasted," because it is perceived as a commodity almost as tangible as physical objects. This monochronic view has helped advance empirical knowledge of the natural world through scientific research. It is a submerged belief (or cluster of beliefs) that is taken for granted in American middle-class society. For that reason, it is not surprising to realize that measuring time becomes a taken-for-granted practice in those (mostly white) congregations growing out of middle-class communities.

Different submerged beliefs about time directly influence expectations about things like worship.

A monochronic assumption of time, however, does not explain the common African American worship practices described on the previous page. These practices and the related artifacts suggest what researchers call a "polychronic" view of time. Around the world, many old societies maintain ways of life that have been based for centuries on this cluster of submerged beliefs. Even the use of the word *time* has to be understood more as "opportunity" than anything else. The rhythms of the natural world all express this view—in birth, growth, and death of individual creatures; in the planting, growth, and harvesting of crops; in patterns of weather. Polychronic communities do not watch the clock, because they originally experienced the world primarily through its natural occurrences and cycles.

In the United States, polychronic communities tend to live "in the shadows" of monochronic communities. In contrast to the dominant white culture's monochronic view, other racial and ethnic groups in America typically represent polychronic views of time—in part reflected in the traditional heritages that they strive to maintain. It should not surprise us, then, to see that African American churches have a number of common artifacts that owe their explanation to polychronic time. Being "on time" does not have the same meaning in most African American churches as it does in most Euro-American churches. Once those of us in the majority society understand this difference, we can begin to appreciate the qualities of faith that this polychronic view expresses. Realizing that something as basic to a church as worship life is heavily influenced by submerged beliefs can shift our insight. It might even give us new ideas for what our congregation's in-between journey might look like.

SPACE

Other kinds of submerged beliefs concern the nature and use of space. Imagine you are visiting a church facility for the first time. You are aware that everything you observe is part of that congregation's artifacts. In one part of the church building, you find a well-lit office with a mahogany desk, credenza, bookshelves and chairs, flat-screen television, state-of-the-art sound system, and so on. Your curiosity is heightened, however, when you notice a crisply written sign on the solid oak door that reads, "Custodian." Later, as you explore the building's basement, you discover in a far back corner—in a dark and dusty area—a small room not much larger than a closet. This room has only one light, hanging from the center of the ceiling on a single wire, a few broken pieces of furniture, and a faded sign on the half-hinged door that reads, "Pastor's Study."

If you found a church like this, what would run through your mind? Confusion? Amusement? Most of us would find it difficult to imagine a congregation allotting its space in this way. We tend to hold deeply-seated convictions about the status and value of church employees that run at odds with the scene just described. Why would the custodian get the best office and the pastor be given the worst space in the build-ing? If this were an actual situation, our likely conclusion would be that the congregation's submerged beliefs about space differ greatly from the most common assumptions.

> *Congregations are much more influenced by*
> *submerged beliefs about space than they realize.*

Submerged beliefs in this category have to do not only with *physical* space; they also include *personal* space.[6] The dominant macroculture in the United States tends to assume that touching another person is prop-er only under certain conditions and in certain ways. Even though these practices have "loosened up" some since the 1960s, we are still aware, for instance, that the way in which we approach strangers is vastly differ-ent from the way we approach close friends or family members. Cross-cultural research, however, reveals that U.S. standards are not universal. In other societies and social groups, persons stand closer together, or touch and gesture at one another in ways that would not be considered "normal" on a typical U.S. street corner or public building. If we focus only on the differing behavior, we will miss the essential insight that the source of these differences is found in deeper, hidden beliefs.

HUMAN RELATIONSHIPS

Finally, let us also think for a moment about how our deeply rooted premises concerning human relationships can and do affect our congre-gations.[7] Consider, for example, the symbolism involved in the differ-ent traditions of church attire. In some denominations, clergy wear garb that sets them off from parishioners and the wider society; the most obvious examples would be Roman Catholic and Episcopal. In other Christian traditions, pastors dress just like everyone else; Church of Christ and many rural working-class church traditions prefer this. In a few other church traditions, the community of faith itself wears clothing that distinguishes it from the wider world in which they live; Anabaptist traditions such as Amish and Mennonite are easy examples here.

All three of these general customs regarding religious dress are marked by particular observable *artifacts*. If you asked people in each of these faith communities the reason for their particular practice, you likely would get an answer that included an *espoused value* of one kind or another. ("It is important to us that . . .") However, the most telling question is: What unspoken assumptions support those specific artifacts?

*Submerged beliefs—even about human
relationships—go even deeper than religious claims.*

For another example, think about how various church traditions regard the role of women. It is only in the last several decades that women have been allowed to seek ordination as pastors—and even then only in certain denominations. Heated debates have transpired (and continue within some traditions) regarding biblical and theological justifications for supporting or denying women's ordination. It is tempting to suppose that the espoused values that get articulated in such debates hold the weight of energy supporting the position. If, however, we listen to culture more deeply, we come to recognize that the espoused positions are more like the tip of an iceberg. For women's ordination—and many other issues—the foundation of the argument rests below the surface, in those rarely spoken, submerged beliefs.

In the debate over women's ordination, submerged beliefs about gender are at play. Such beliefs, as we have seen already, are not based in religion but rather influence religion. Some segments of U.S. society, for instance, would accept without question a statement like this one: "The obvious biological differences between men and women represent absolute and undeniable distinctions in their respective social roles." This statement represents one kind of deep-seated conviction about human relationships. It could help explain much of the historical and traditional ways in which men and women have been expected to relate with one another.

Yet, in the wake of scientific, medical, and technological developments, other segments of our society argue that women and men should have equal opportunities in the public arena. Even for this opposing position, however, the espoused values articulated to make such a case do not tell the whole story. A submerged belief makes the difference—although clarity about such beliefs rarely surfaces: "Gender has nothing to do with an individual's capacity for being involved in work and community contributions." Even if a deeply held conviction like this might get named aloud eventually, it typically is expressed only dimly.

Submerged Beliefs and Your In-Between Times

This chapter has introduced a number of ideas and terms that probably were not familiar to you. As the writers of the book, we expected that! It is still not common for most people to think about the lives of our faith communities in terms of culture—especially as we dig below the level of things that are observable (artifacts) and desirable (espoused values). Yet benign ignorance will not help your church during its in-between times! There is more energy within your congregation than you realize. Learning how to understand the complex character of this energy is one crucial way to help your church in the long run.

What makes this kind of digging into culture so valuable is that it can illuminate the roots of difference, of opportunity, and of inertia. As your congregation becomes accustomed to paying attention to what is being uncovered, a host of new insights will occur. You will begin to understand why certain church members and groups are more interested than others in particular activities or facilities. You will begin to appreciate the ways in which your church is like its immediate community—as well as how it is different in some respects. You will be more effective in evaluating new ideas. Perhaps even more crucially, you will become more adept at anticipating where your congregation is likely to see results—and where your submerged beliefs could act as roadblocks.

Submerged beliefs become the key to navigating and negotiating all of the church's challenges of being in between. In-between times can create within the congregation nervousness and might spark the elements of conflict. This is natural and normal, but becoming hampered by these feelings is not necessary. As it learns to identify and deal with its deep-seated premises, your congregation can learn to channel and use energy generated from tension. We use the term *learn* purposefully; such learning is deliberate and conscious, because it involves a way of thinking about your church that is not familiar.

*Submerged beliefs become the key to navigating
and negotiating all of the church's challenges of
being in between.*

We encourage you to review the examples and illustrations in this chapter as you consider what you are learning about your congregation's submerged beliefs and their importance. As you will see in the next chapter, your in-between times are influenced by yet another basic element of culture. This element—which we will call "lifecycle"—interacts with your submerged beliefs, affecting your congregation's ability to respond to change. A congregation's in-between times can generate both threat and opportunity. The lifecycle framework described in the next chapter will help you be less surprised by the undertow that could hit you.

Spiritual Practice

In order to begin to discover the deep energy of your church, you will want to create a safe space where there is no value judgment placed on any of your group's discoveries. Rather than beginning with things that take away energy, the following spiritual practice offers you time to appreciate the best of who you have been as a congregation as you continue your journey toward God's preferred future. Your conversation will be one of appreciation and gratitude, using the Appreciative Inquiry Model discussed by Mark Lau Branson in *Memories, Hopes, and Conversations*.[8]

As you sit in a circle together, have the group divide into pairs. After reading the following three questions, each individual should share his or her answers with the other person. Take turns and make a few notes on what you hear.

Speak only in terms of gratitude (no negativity here, stay positive)! Here are the questions:

1. Remembering your entire experience at this church, when were you most alive, most motivated, and most excited about your involvement? What made it exciting? Who else was involved? What happened? What was your part? Describe how you felt.
2. What do you value most about our church? What are its best features?
3. What three wishes do you have for the future of our church?

After the partners have listened to one another, sit in silence until the entire group is ready. When your *guide* for this practice invites you to respond, begin by giving thanks for what you have learned from one another, and then share what you have heard with the entire group.

Your *guide* can take notes on a large sheet of paper, so that your stories of gratitude may be noted.

When everyone has shared words of appreciation, we invite you to offer your gratitude to God as you pray these words together:

Ever-creating and re-creating God, we are grateful.
The sighs, the tears, the memories shared remind us
of your faithfulness and your call on our common life.
We do not want to dwell on the "good old days,"
yet we do want to bring the best of who we have been
into your call on our future.
Guide us in this in-between time
as we seek to discover a fresh vision
that will lead us into vital witness.
In the name of the One who calls and leads, we pray. Amen.

5 Discovering Treasure: What Could Your Church Become?

Six days later, Jesus took with him Peter and James and John, and led them up a high mountain apart, by themselves. And he was transfigured before them, and his clothes became dazzling white, such as no one on earth could bleach them. And there appeared to them Elijah with Moses, who were talking with Jesus. Then Peter said to Jesus, "Rabbi, it is good for us to be here; let us make three dwellings, one for you, one for Moses, and one for Elijah." He did not know what to say, for they were terrified. Then a cloud overshadowed them, and from the cloud there came a voice, "This is my Son, the Beloved; listen to him!" Suddenly when they looked around, they saw no one with them any more, but only Jesus.

As they were coming down the mountain, he ordered them to tell no one about what they had seen, until after the Son of Man had risen from the dead.

—Mark 9:2–9

Over the centuries, one of the church's favorite stories about Jesus has been his transfiguration. You remember the story: Jesus takes Peter, James, and John with him up to "a high mountain," away from the crowds who have been pressing upon Jesus. During this time, he had been busy in his teaching, preaching, and healing; the Twelve were traveling with him and doing ministry as well. Matthew, Mark, and Luke tell the story similarly (Matt. 17:1–8; Mark 9:2–8; Luke 9:28–36), with minor differences in detail. Luke says that they went to pray (Luke 9:28), a practice Luke frequently emphasizes for his main characters. We can understand that, with the demands on him growing, Jesus would want to rest and keep his spiritual balance.

It is easy to imagine that these three men who accompanied Jesus on this quick retreat thought of themselves as extra special. Peter figures prominently in a number of Gospel episodes, and James and John once asked their Lord to give them special places in his kingdom (Mark 10:35–45; also Matt. 20:20–28, where the brothers' mother makes this request for them!). The other nine must have been back with "the disciples," the larger entourage of men and women who had left their homes to follow Jesus on his ministry journeys. Perhaps Peter, James, and John expected that this mountain trek might demonstrate how privileged they were.

If so, they surely were not disappointed—at least, not at first. In Jesus's day, Moses was a figure larger than life—the leader of the exodus and deliverer of the Ten Commandments. The prophet Elijah also held special status—and was an object of wonderment—because he had been taken up into heaven on a whirlwind (2 Kings 2:1–12). It was said that Elijah would return one day—but when, and under what circumstances? In Jesus's day, questions like these must have been on the minds of every Jew who knew the stories of their ancestors. Moses and Elijah still enjoyed rock-star status—and suddenly there they were, talking with Jesus, the leader of a new religious revival.

If we read this biblical story too quickly, we will fail to appreciate it fully. The vision of their ancestral heroes on the same "stage" with their movement's leader astounded Peter, James, and John. "Dumbfounded" is probably more like it; in the Bible, fear, awe, and astonishment are often closely linked. Even Jesus himself looked completely different— the description of his appearance goes to great lengths to present the itinerant preacher in celestial status. These three lucky ducks were privy to a vision that certainly must have scrambled their understandings of what this Jesus movement was all about. Peter, true to form, pipes up first, offering at least a feeble attempt to acknowledge the climactic nature of the moment. Then he suggests that they all hang around on the mountain for a while, and that they construct "tents" for each of the religious leaders—as though it were possible to freeze the glory of the moment indefinitely.

The story would have had great dramatic punch even if it had ended right there—but it does not. A rapidly-moving scene, beginning with a cloud and a mysterious voice, puts the episode over the top. It is as if God wanted to make sure that Peter, James, and John got the point: "Here is the guy! So pay attention to what he has to say!" Then, just as quickly as it all had transpired, the party was over—no time for autographs, pictures, or interviews. To top it off, these three stunned witnesses to this epiphany go mute about it. In Mark (8:9) and Matthew (17:9), Jesus tells them not to say anything; in Luke (9:36), the text implies that Peter, James, and John decide among themselves to keep the whole thing under wraps.

Talk about a roller-coaster ride—these guys just had one! We know that sojourning to the mountains is a biblical symbol of spiritual and divine focusing—nothing like a simple stroll in the park. Yet it would have been difficult—don't you think?—for Peter, James, and John to have wondered what could happen next. Wasn't this about as good as it gets? Visions of such magnitude appear once in a blue moon, and who can see them coming? "Darn, too bad Jesus didn't go for the tent thing; we could have stayed up there a long time and reveled in the glory of it!"

For the two of us, Jesus's transfiguration story has become a metaphor of the dangers facing churches that find themselves in between. Over the years, churches can be tempted to allow their identities to get stuck on some "high point" from their past. A superlative experience, a particular pastor's tenure, or a celebrated achievement comes to represent the congregation's crowning moment. It is as though the members believe they have reached the mountaintop already, and that the future will offer nothing better. Like Peter, James, and John, our churches can be wowed by the pizzazz of an exciting experience or a stirring story from their past and then try to hold on to it—to ride its coattails. When this happens, the congregation's attitude shifts. What *used to* be becomes more interesting than what *could* be.

> *It is tempting for your church to get stuck on some*
> *"high point" from its past.*

Jesus came down the mountain after the cloud cleared, and his appearance returned to normal. He did not take Peter up on his offer to stay up there. This refusal suggests an insight of spiritual significance. In spite of the moment of glory there, Jesus knew that neither he nor his followers would serve God's purposes best by getting stuck on a high. There was more to do, more to prepare for, more to learn. We cannot stay atop the mountain forever, ride the wave for more than a few seconds, or stand in the winner's circle long after the photographers leave.

Throughout this book, we have emphasized that all churches inevitably face periods in their lives in which they find themselves "in between." The temptation at this point is to try to stay up on the mountain, to build those three tents even after Moses and Elijah have disappeared and Jesus is halfway back down the trail. It is our purpose in this chapter to understand why this tendency arises. While it is both common and natural, if this temptation is not overcome, it can hurt your church.

As pastors, teachers, and coaches, we have found it illuminating to imagine communities of faith as going through stages of a lifecycle. In its earliest years, everything a church does must be focused on the immediate future, on making things happen rather quickly. Gradually—over weeks, months, and then its early years—a congregation achieves something of the kind of results for which it has hoped; it creates its own distinctiveness and momentum. This momentum allows it, over another phase of experiences, to build a functional balance between stability and new possibilities. At some point (if all goes well!), the church will hit a peak, a high point of achievement that even could exceed what it previously had imagined. From there, the greatest danger is that the church will try to coast, to rest on its laurels, to maintain familiar programs and relationships at the expense of considering new possibilities. If this "autopilot" mode continues (as it usually does), eventually the church will lose effectiveness. The membership will grow older; fewer younger families and children will be present; the facilities will begin to look neglected. At some point, the decline becomes too obvious to ignore, but efforts to turn things around are not as easy as anyone hopes. Crises and open conflicts erode the congregation's capacity to respond. Yet it may still be a number of years before the few remaining members decide, from among their limited options, what to do. The death of a congregation is often slow and painful.

This quick overview of congregational lifecycle describes phases that usually occur over a number of decades. Understanding this notion of lifecycle can help churches realize right away that "in-between times" are not the exception; rather, they are typical. Few church members have enough history with their congregation to appreciate its ups and downs, its ins and outs, the fullness of its journey. Even those congregations that pass on detailed histories (whether oral or written) usually give those stories no more than a superficial interpretation ("Things were good then," "That was a rough period for us," etc.). In other words, it is not easy to decipher the current moment of your congregation's life within its larger flow of experience. By understanding your congregation's journey in terms of lifecycle, you open the door to a world of rich, unexpected insight. You begin to realize that a church being "in between" is much more common than anyone typically acknowledges. As teachers and coaches, it is our hope that the framework of lifecycle helps to normalize your church's experience of being "in between."

In-between times are not the exception;
rather, they are typical.

So, begin by asking yourselves: *What treasure is hidden for our church to discover, if we give attention to the normal and natural phases that every church experiences?*

And then ask: *What possibilities will these discoveries offer us as we lean into our time in between?*

The Four Phases of Your Church's Lifecycle

Many of the issues that your church has faced or will face are triggered by its journey through its lifecycle. By understanding this framework, your church is better prepared to look for treasure rather than trouble.

For our purposes, it will be enough to talk about four basic lifecycle phases and the kinds of "in-between" issues that each one creates.

In-between times can be predicted as churches go through one or another of four basic lifecycle phases: *up-and-coming, dynamic, established,* and *weakening.*[1] In each of these phases, particular challenges and opportunities present themselves. While the "feel" of being in-between is hardest to detect in the "established" phase, all four phases deal with transitions of one kind or another. Additionally, each phase leads to a different relationship between the basic elements of the church's cultural pond. The questions, uncertainties, and struggles that are typical and normal in each phase connect what seems obvious with the deeper dimensions of your church's culture. These dimensions are more fluid—in the long run—than one might think. Shifts in artifacts and espoused values represent more than what appears on the surface.

Having now introduced the lifecycle model and its usefulness to churches, let us look more closely at each of the phases.[2]

Up-and-Coming

Like any new business, agency, nonprofit, school, or other organization, every community of faith has a starting point. Congregations begin in a particular place, at a particular time, with a particular group of people. A church might start out as a Bible study in someone's home; it might be formed by a group of immigrants that wants to maintain its religious tradition as it begins life in a new country; it might start with five acres of prime property and funding from a denomination; it might have split off from another church over a disagreement; it might have been founded by a courageous minister who spent a lifetime establishing new congregations in a frontier land.

However your congregation was born—whether it was two years ago or two centuries ago—it began its life facing a predictable set of issues that had to be handled effectively. In general terms, these issues concern enough people, adequate resources, and satisfactory achievements. In other words, whatever a new church's vision might be, there also are a few other basic issues to which it must attend, if the venture is to succeed. One of these issues is people, in sufficient numbers to do what the new congregation says it wants to do. Another one of these issues is enough space, facilities, and skills at hand (resources). If these two broad categories do not get handled well, the third one—satisfactory achievement—is not likely to be met either.

Suppose a new congregation is established to reach the generation of young adults moving into a certain community. Research on today's new adults shows this generation does not go to church out of duty, that they look for meaning, that they are unlike their baby boomer parents, and so on.[3] If the first members of this new congregation are concerned primarily about having traditional hymnbooks, choirs with robes, and finding a building that "looks like a church," they are unlikely to attract a critical mass of potential new members. In this case, the vision may be appropriate, but the skills (as resources) for making basic decisions in the start-up are not on target. This new congregation could struggle and might not make it (insufficient achievement), even if it has sufficient money and space.

The up-and-coming phase, however, deals with more than simply getting a new congregation started. There is no guarantee that a brand-new church will survive. It takes time to build momentum—with effective activities (worship, nurture, community-building, service, etc.) that generate ongoing enthusiasm, commitment, and support. New churches might have lots of energy but not much staying power. With little history, they are capable of turning on a dime, changing what they are doing fairly quickly. The question is: Can they sustain themselves for the long haul?

For an up-and-coming congregation, then, just about *everything* is transition! In simple terms, the principal word to describe the up-and-coming church's life is *what*. When you are just beginning, you can't merely talk about doing something; you have to *do* it! There are many decisions to make regarding activities, events, and programs; little of what goes on seems set in stone; focus has to remain more on the future than on what has happened already; one of the big challenges is maintaining energy and willingness to keep at it. The congregation's history—and its culture—is emerging, from all of the young church's experiences and perceptions. Committed members and staff realize that the young congregation is somewhere "in between" birth and stability. With continued achievement and a sense of satisfaction among members over time, the up-and-coming church eventually can move through this phase successfully.

*For up-and-coming churches, the descriptive word
is* what—*What activities, events, and programs
best represent pursuit of their mission?*

For the majority of our readers, however, we realize that what we
have just described is probably not very relevant. Most of you who read
this book are likely *not* part of a church that is up-and-coming. Few
congregations in the U.S. today find themselves in this phase of organizational lifecycle. For the old-line Protestant denominations, up-and-
coming churches are known as "new church developments," "start-up
congregations," and the like. Number-wise, they are small—most likely
less than 5 percent of our total congregational count. Still, these older
denominations have been seeking in recent years to establish more new
congregations. There is a certain glamour about them—they are fresh,
exciting, full of promise. Yet a congregation cannot stay in the up-and-
coming phase forever. If it survives, it will move inevitably into another
lifecycle phase. This means the church will face new kinds of transitions, requiring different kinds of responses. The glamour will wear off,
and the young congregation will struggle to find its way amid seemingly
competing demands.

Dynamic

No, not every new congregation survives. The many challenges repre-
sented by numbers (human and otherwise) and achievements do not
disappear automatically after one exciting Easter service or the comple-
tion of the congregation's first facility. Challenges can remain unmet,
or can be handled in ways that cause conflict to erupt. Not every young
church that survives does so with positive strength. (We will discuss this
unfortunate-but-not-infrequent phenomenon in the text that follows.)
For those who do survive, however, the dynamic phase dawns as a moment of sweet payoff.

A congregation in the dynamic phase is firing on all pistons and
seeing results that exceed their expectations. Although the members often cannot explain why, dynamic churches have found a way to refocus
themselves and increase their efficiency. That is, they not only have a
fresh sense of their vision, but they also have put processes in place that
are less likely to burn out people and burn up resources. Activities and

programs are working well; members are upbeat, motivated, and willing to learn; there is ease in talking about the church's ministry in light of its context; and operational processes support, rather than complicate, the church's life and witness. As an organization, the dynamic church has found its own way to maintain a creative tension between continuity and flexibility. Of the four phases, dynamic is at the peak; it is the one that we hope our churches attain, maintain, or regain. The importance of this point will become more evident by the end of this chapter.

Dynamic congregations can be mostly quickly and easily described in one simple word: *why*. Their vision is clear, articulated, and compelling—that is, their purpose, their "why," drives everything else. Their decisions about programs and activities ("what"), nurturing of relationships and connectedness ("who"—more below), patterns of resource use and support mechanisms ("how"—more below) all remain guided by and accountable to the congregation's vision. It typically takes a number of years for any church to get to this point, especially since "why" and "who" take time and intention to be developed effectively. Of the four functions just named here, "why" and "who" cannot be forced or rushed.[4]

> *"Why" is the driving function of the dynamic*
> *church—its energy flows out of its vision.*

Churches in the dynamic phase feel a little like that episode in which Peter, James, and John witnessed Jesus transfigured on the mountain. Jesus's movement was formed already, and the band of followers had accompanied Jesus to several locations around their region. Jesus had taught, preached, and healed many and had sent some of Jesus's followers out on missions to do the same. Large crowds had gathered; his popularity had grown to the point where religious authorities were beginning to be concerned about this upstart prophet and his followers.

By the time, then, that Jesus trekked up the mountain with the three, this up-and-coming movement he had organized was well on its way. Those dramatic moments with Moses and Elijah stand as a symbol of the dynamic phase. The experience is capped off by the voice from the cloud, which encapsulates the purpose of—the vision for—Jesus's ministry. Like Peter, James, and John's mountaintop experience, the dynamic phase can have almost a euphoric effect upon congregants. It is so rewarding to witness such satisfying results that church members (and pastors!) often feel a sense of arrival: "This is as good as it gets! So let's stay right here, doing what we are doing now (and build the booths for that purpose), so we can maintain this feeling always."

From a lifecycle standpoint, Jesus's heading right back down the mountain creates more symbolism—this time, ironic. We will see below that churches moving beyond the dynamic phase indicates a loss of flexibility, during which maintaining the status quo becomes of primary interest. This decreasing concern for staying adaptable is like passing the crest of a mountain and then going downhill. Symbolically, this is what happens to churches past the dynamic phase. However, in the case of the transfiguration story, descending the mountain has almost the opposite function. It is as if Jesus knew the danger of staying high, of resting on top, of reveling too long in a glorious moment. Heading down the mountain was Jesus's way of demonstrating that his movement needed to remain dynamic: If an elite few celebrated too long, the movement would begin to decline, and its purpose would suffer.

The biggest danger to a church in the dynamic stage is that it will begin to coast. Resting on one's laurels seems to be a common tendency in human experience, both individually and collectively. Jesus's refusal to stay on the high mountain symbolizes a recognition that churches cannot remain dynamic if they try to hold onto what they cherish the most. Being dynamic is not characterized by a particular set of achievements but by a style of openness to the Spirit that permeates the congregation. The necessity of flexibility cannot be overlooked or bypassed.

From our years of pastoral experience and research, we have come to a pair of sobering conclusions about the dynamic lifecycle phase. One, there are not many churches that are in it. Two, those churches that are in the dynamic phase don't stay there long. The lure of comfortable practices and familiar relationships pulls strongly. Moving from a stance of creative accomplishment into a phase marked by habitual routines and associations usually occurs slowly and subtly, to the point that those on the inside don't even realize it has happened. There is more irony here, since the dynamic phase can help congregations see that transition is normal and they can learn to live with it.

We state this point again: One of the most important insights for twenty-first-century churches to learn is that being "in between" is typical, not unusual. We have few illusions about how dramatic and difficult it can be for congregations to wrap their minds around this point. However, in today's world, the attitude of clinging to what is comfortable can lead gradually to irrelevance and a slow, painful institutional death.

It doesn't have to be this way! Your church can learn to pay attention, to face those internal and external elements that might seem scary, to lean into the seeming uncertainty of being between what you know and what you might not want to know. For our purposes in this chapter, it is of central importance to realize that the dynamic lifecycle stage in the lifecycle is how you want your congregation to learn to live. Yes, to do so will involve time, energy, and struggle—but the blessings for ministry will be significant and far-reaching.

Again, the dynamic phase is most desirable for churches, but it is not that common today. Much more frequently, churches spend more of their lives in the next phase—established.

Established

As we have implied in the previous section, churches typically do not recognize they have entered a lifecycle transition until its effects become noticeable. Usually, the effects of such transition are viewed negatively, perhaps even fearfully or angrily. The one exception might be the lifecycle transition from the dynamic into the established phase. Such a transition does not occur quickly, in a day or a month; rather, it emerges over a longer period of time and almost imperceptibly. Within any organization, satisfaction with the achievements of the dynamic phase can feed a growing sense that the organization has "arrived." If enough key persons in the organization share this feeling, their decisions will influence the actions and attitudes of the organization as a whole. Like any other organization, churches are just as susceptible to sliding into complacence.

Some congregations with a long history like to refer to a "golden age" in their past, when the church built its current sanctuary, or benefited from a long-tenured pastor, or played a major role regarding key issues in the community. There is nothing wrong with such stories! They often indeed capture moments in a congregation's life in which vision, energy, adaptability, and achievement came together in remarkable new ways. The established church, however, uses the stories told about its past to revel in the way things used to be. Such attention to the past points to diminishing congregational focus on its future (dynamic).

The temptation to rest in past accomplishments becomes even more seductive because all of the most obvious signs of "growth" continue. The established congregation—early in the phase—can point to comparable membership, worship, and education attendance records and similar budget and finance numbers over recent years as key indicators that justify its "staying the course." At this point, the church's vision is politely acknowledged but not thoughtfully engaged. This diminished attention to vision then creates the complacence that sees no need for trying new things. Flexibility is gradually sacrificed, often with the attitude of "If it's not broken, why fix it?"

For a church in the established phase, this attitude marks the beginning of its steady decline. Early on, an established church typically believes it is successful enough that it does not need to deal with any changes around it. It has not yet seen any significant decline in people or resources. It is hard for congregations at this point to realize they never have the luxury of controlling the basic features of their context, those that permit their existence.

Because established churches are satisfied, they do not expect that changing circumstances will throw them a curveball. In this particular organizational culture, it seems that all transitions have been met and conquered. They have reached the Promised Land; it is abundance and ease from now on. Sometimes a new member will suggest a new idea for ministry, only to be met with tepid interest. If the new idea fits into an existing scheme, it might fly; otherwise, it often dies by neglect. New members can become frustrated that such a resourceful congregation seems blind to spiritual needs and ministry opportunities.

This scenario also points out what happens to relationships within established congregations. In the dynamic phase—when vision is still strong—it is easy for a church to welcome new people and their gifts: The congregation's vision is more compelling at this point than the strength of any particular network of people. As a church slides out of *dynamic* and into *established*, the energy once focused on vision moves toward networks and relationships. Cliques of various kinds form, creating support, security, and power for some people but decreasing connectedness for others. For this reason, as we call up-and-coming the "what" phase and dynamic the "why" phase, we call established the "who" phase.

*The primary focus of the church in the
established phase is "who"—relationships, cliques,
and their respective powers.*

We seek here to present a picture of the established church that is both honest and realistic, showing both its strengths and its dangers. Perhaps one way to articulate these dangers is by saying that the "established" church believes it has reached the top of a mountain where it can remain indefinitely. From the perspective of lifecycle, however, we receive the key insight that congregational life is not static. Neither life nor faith stands still; there is plenty of witness in the Scriptures to this truism. Any congregation that seeks to coast along on the strength of past accomplishments will discover eventually that the world has passed them by. The failure to pay attention to circumstances that create times of being "in between" is a clear pitfall of the established phase.

There is one other main point about the established phase that bears directly upon a church's grace for the journey. This concerns how churches enter this phase—and, while hard to hear, this point is significant. As the discussion above indicates, many churches move from dynamic into established; they experience a period of vitality before drifting into a complacent (although still fairly effective) mode. However, this is not the path every church ends up taking. In our study of congregations, the two of us have discovered that some churches do not move from up-and-coming to dynamic. Instead, difficult situations that did not work out well in the first phase can be so harmful as to trigger the church into an early decline.

In other words, rather than learning to thrive from its decisions and actions, an up-and-coming church always runs the innate risk of being crippled by them. It might experience a split over some issue or an action the pastor took; the church might suffer a major financial crisis; a few key founding members might receive job transfers; the board and/or members might not be able to agree on how to respond to a basic opportunity, either within the congregation (programming) or beyond it (outreach). Developments such as these call for clarity of purpose and mutual commitment—fundamental factors that up-and-coming churches are still identifying and testing. If it cannot manage the tension through to a constructive resolution, the young, fragile congregation could fall apart. If it does find a way to hang in there, the church can survive. However, in these cases, the drive to survive has taken on such a priority that it could drain the congregation. As a result, the predictable and necessary transition issues that would have carried the church into the dynamic phase never get addressed.

This scenario—in which a young church suddenly ends up in a premature established phase—is more common than you might think. As teachers, we have heard far too many stories from seminary students about congregations that are limping along. Somewhere in the church's past lurks a painful, debilitating episode from its early days. Such stories typically are not mentioned in public, but old-timers know them and perhaps were players in them. At some level, they realize that something had disrupted the congregation's development. As a result, that internal dissension led to the creation of submerged beliefs that emphasize security and reticence over adventure and confidence.

So, what do "prematurely established" congregations feel when they discover they have entered in-between waters? Their tendency is to hunker down, to avoid talking about it (because "when we talk together, we end up fighting"), and to ignore, isolate, or even expel those who keep bringing up the situation. For them, being in between is not a good thing! There is little in their chest of submerged beliefs that leads them to believe they can benefit from working through the issues that the transition presents them with.

> *Every established congregation faces the threat of a*
> *gradual slide into the weakening phase.*

"Prematurely established" congregations are especially susceptible to declining into the last lifecycle phase. Actually, every established congregation faces the threat of a gradual slide down the lifecycle into the weakening phase. In this book, we are asserting that congregational decline, as a result of in-between times, is typical but not inevitable. In order to be well equipped for avoiding such a slide, congregations do well to understand what awaits them. Grace for the journey does not require ignorance of one's circumstances!

Weakening

For many, if not most, churches in the weakening phase, there is no common awareness of having arrived there. The core of submerged beliefs that developed in the up-and-coming phase still rules the congregation's life—hidden from plain sight (as they always are), but strong and pervasive nonetheless. In fact, it is the persistence of particular submerged beliefs that explains the church's weakened condition. As we discussed in chapter 4, submerged beliefs develop early in the congregation's life, in response to the various issues and decisions that it has to make. However, the conditions with which the young church interacted during its earliest days will change over the intervening years.

This point is one of the keys to understanding in-between times. Yes, there will be occasions when your church's transition emerges from something internal—such as the resignation of a pastor, the death of a key longtime member, or an electrical fire in the sanctuary. Yet, more often than not, a church is prone to being caught off guard by the consequences of external changes—one or more of a host of demographic and related shifts over which the church has virtually no control. (One way we recommend watching for those changes is through the lens of "cultural confluence"; again, see chapter 3, "Cocoons and the Internet.") One way or another, the world that supported the "success" of those early submerged beliefs is changing. However, in spite of those changes, most established churches continue with business as usual. Such a common strategy will lead them—even if not immediately—into a weakening condition.

A weakening congregation does not realize that its deepest cultural energy is losing its capacity for keeping the church strong. The rules of the world around it are in flux, but the weakening church is unable to acknowledge that it is not ready to respond. What makes this phase distinct from its lifecycle predecessor is twofold: one, the relative loss of strength and, two, a shift in major function. Most weakening congregations have been losing members for a number of years, especially younger adults and families with young children. The members who remain often have moved out of the neighborhood and are driving farther to get to the church's facilities. The building itself is almost revered but is showing signs of age and benign neglect. The surrounding neighborhood no longer supports the same population from which the church first drew most of its members.

Sometimes, it is necessary to stand back and get a larger view in order to appreciate the integral ties between congregation and context. For instance, our combined experience as pastors has made us familiar with many of the demographic features of both metro Atlanta and

Chicagoland. Ethnicity, class, and race continue to play major roles—as they have for many decades—in the shifting realities of urban neighborhoods. Even small towns and rural areas today feel these effects, even if not as quickly or extensively. If your church entered the established phase before any of these realities began shifting around you, it would not be surprising to find that your church has moved into the weakening phase.

> *The descriptive word in the weakening*
> *phase is* how—*as in, how will the congregation*
> *sustain a diminished number of comfortable*
> *activities and processes.*

Our simple word for distinguishing the weakening phase from the other three phases is *how*. No longer is the congregation driven by the momentum of its past and the tight networks of "who." Any public appeal to "why" has faded away; decisions about "what" have long been settled. Now, the church runs almost on autopilot: of central importance is *how* things happen—in worship, in the few remaining programs and activities, in maintenance and finance. This is the life of an organization that hopes it can ride out whatever led to its survival mentality.

To outsiders, a weakening congregation is often a sad phenomenon to witness, especially if these observers have the patience to sympathize. However, for the remnant who remain, this lackluster congregation is still their spiritual home. It has survived the years, almost in spite of its reluctance (even refusal?) to explore ways to be faithful in a new day. Still, the weakening church is already in an in-between time. So, here is the hard-nosed truth: The sooner the weakening church accepts this reality, the better chance it has of doing something positive about it. Churches in the weakening phase have almost completely lost the ability to respond to change. Grace for its journey is released when the congregation's current truth can be spoken in its midst.

> *Churches in the weakening phase have almost*
> *completely lost the ability to respond to change.*

Facing Today's In-Between Times

Lifecycle interpretation of congregations provides one key benchmark for understanding the challenges and promise of in-between times. Transitional moments that a church faces might appear to be minor and easily manageable, but locating them in the church's current lifecycle phase begins to draw out their complexity. It is tempting to suppose that in-between times and lifecycle decline can be dealt with as quickly and easily as changing your car's oil or replacing a worn-out window air conditioner. Wrong! The work calls for significant energy, focus, and time. As a tool of analysis, lifecycle (like confluence, and the cultural pond) allows for truth-telling and establishes a framework for taking action.

It is important, for instance, to recognize that an analysis of all existing congregations would locate them somewhere across the four phases. As we have suggested already, it is not an even distribution. Based on our years of research and observation, it appears that there are many more congregations in the two "declining" phases (established and weakening) than in the two "growing" phases (up-and-coming and dynamic). This broad conclusion applies especially to older mainline denominations, those traditions that were formed more than a century ago. Many thousands of congregations and parishes that were established before 1900 are discovering that the assumptions and approaches that allowed them to flourish in the 1950s world will not sustain them in the twenty-first century. Countless national and international developments since World War II alone have transformed our social, cultural, and economic landscape. Over the last few decades, the familiar comforts of life in the established phase have been giving way to quiet survival. This is a growing and persistent phenomenon, making transition an increasingly common issue for many churches.

We estimate that at least three-fourths of those U.S. congregations that are more than a century old are now on the lifecycle decline; among them, the weight perhaps has shifted now, more to the weakening phase. This means that a much smaller percentage of churches exist in either the up-and-coming or dynamic phase. It is fairly easy to identify up-and-coming churches: They are characterized by few years of existence, a tendency to attract younger people, a strong sense of focus and energy, a willingness to try new ideas, and less attachment to specific space and stuff. Virtually all mainline denominations seem committed to encouraging more up-and-coming congregations—partly due to years of declining membership totals. In the up-and-coming lifecycle phase, it is much easier to deal with being in between, since a start-up has no history or stability.

As for the dynamic phase, we are dealing with an even smaller percentage. The description of dynamic churches earlier in the chapter suggests why this is the case. Our natural human tendency is to seek stability and then try to maintain all of its familiar and comfortable forms. Stability is not a bad thing in and of itself. In the long run, however, failure to deal effectively with changes around us does lead eventually to institutional decline and irrelevance. There are plenty of examples—in history, politics, business, and religion—to illustrate this point.

Perhaps the single most vital message that a lifecycle perspective offers is that churches should seek to attain, sustain, or regain the dynamic phase. This task calls for churches to have the capacity and willingness to be responsive to changes in and around them. Congregations will be unable to do so, however, unless they are willing to recognize and lean into the uncertainties of in-between times. How to embrace the grace of such inevitable moments is the subject of the final chapter.

Spiritual Practice

In the introduction, as we first joined you on your journey, we suggested that you pray through the prophetic words offered in Isaiah 43:1–4. Now, as you consider where your congregation finds itself on the life-cycle, we invite you to visit another passage from later in the same chapter of Isaiah.

Center your focus on these words from Isaiah 43:18–21 as your *guide* reads them aloud:

> Do not remember the former things
> or consider the things of old.
> I am about to do a new thing;
> now it springs forth, Do you not perceive it?
> I will make a way in the wilderness
> and rivers in the desert . . .
> for I give water in the wilderness,
> rivers in the desert,
> to give drink to my chosen people . . .
> so that they might declare my praise.

Often, when congregations come face to face with their weakening state, they become listless. Fatigue and anxiety replace hope and energy. Small groups such as the choir, youth ministry, women's group, and others, vie for what they need to survive. Tunnel vision prevails and imagination is impossible. "We've always done it this way" becomes the mantra of the day. Voices are silenced by anxiety.

Communities of faith, who find their churches in decline, forget the promises of YHWH offered in the prophetic words; instead, a scarcity mentality abounds.

"How will we survive if . . . ?" replaces "I am about to do a new thing."

Though it is easy to forget, we are a resurrection people, waiting for God's "new thing."

We believe your church can experience resurrection as a dynamic congregation.

And through this spiritual practice we invite you to imagine the possibilities.

Seated in your circle once more, close your eyes and let go of the cares and worries of this day. Be present in this moment, aware that you are not alone.

Remember the thoughts and feelings of gratitude you offered in the spiritual practice of Appreciative Inquiry you shared together at the end of chapter 4.

After a few moments, open your eyes and look at one another as you sit with those feelings.

Then read aloud these words from Isaiah again:

Do not remember the former things . . .
I am about to do a new thing; . . .
do you not perceive it? . . .
for I will give water in the wilderness,
rivers in the desert
to give drink to my chosen people,
so that they might declare my praise.

Now begin to reflect on these questions:

- How can we let go of those things that keep us tied to our past rather than helping us become more responsive to change?
- Do we believe God is calling this church into a new life?
- What is the wilderness place in our church that is thirsty?
- What is one thing we might do as a congregation to allow God to fill that thirst?

Sit in silence for ten seconds.

One by one each person will invite another member of the group by name to share his or her reflections. Allow ten seconds of silence after each person has spoken before inviting another to share.

If persons choose not to accept the invitation to share at this time, that is their choice. If someone chooses not to speak, thank him or her, and invite another person, by name, to share.

Value each reflection with gratitude, without judgment or agreement. *Remember to honor the ten seconds of silence following each reflection.*

After each person has had the opportunity to share, you may ask for clarification from one another and begin to dialogue about God's grace-filled possibilities.[5]

Close your time together with your sentence prayers of praise and thanksgiving.

6 No Surprises Please: Engaging Natural Resistance

So the LORD said to Moses, "Gather for me seventy of the elders of Israel, . . . And say to the people: Consecrate yourselves for tomorrow, and you shall eat meat; for you have wailed in the hearing of the LORD, saying, 'If only we had to meat to eat! Surely it was better for us in Egypt.' Therefore the LORD will give you meat, and you shall eat. You shall eat not only one day, or two days, or five days, or ten days, or twenty days, but for a whole month—until it comes out of your nostrils and becomes loathsome to you—because you have rejected the LORD who is among you, and have wailed before him, saying, 'Why did we ever leave Egypt?'"

—Numbers 11:16–20

We believe that God has a sense of humor!

There is a little story way back in the Hebrew Bible that gives us an early glimpse into the ways of God with our spiritual ancestors. This wilderness episode is tucked into a portion of the Pentateuch (the first five books of the Bible) that most of us would read only if we had to do so. The book of Numbers deals a lot with two censuses that were taken— one when the Israelites were still fresh from their escape of Egypt, and another after the first generation had died off. Our story of interest opens an abruptly introduced section of Numbers, in which the Israelites are complaining about their circumstances (11:1).[1]

Complaining? Complaining! A bit ironic—don't you think? This band of Jacob's ancestors has just escaped slavery in Egypt and won-drously passed through the Red Sea, watching their pursuers perish. They hardly have had time to catch their breath before some folks in their party begin complaining about the food they have to eat in the wilderness (manna). These dissidents' description of their diet in Egypt (Num. 11:5) would have sounded pretty tasty to ancient Mediterranean ears. No wonder they might have been a bit wistful—although I ques-tion their accuracy on this point!

Hmm. Does anyone see the irony in this? The Israelites are now free, because of God's action on their behalf. In virtually no time, however, they have begun to complain about their diet on the journey—a staple that God is providing for their benefit. I can almost hear God between the lines of the text: *"Who saved you from those harsh conditions?"* *"Who is giving you enough to eat every day, while you are traveling through this dangerous desert?"* What makes the story even more believable is the mention of "rabble among them," apparently a small group of trouble-makers who were especially hard to please. This group "had a strong craving" (v. 4) that stirred up the rest of the folks in the camp, causing them to wail and talk as though their life in Egypt was wonderful.

Are you chuckling yet? If you have not sensed the ironic humor in this story yet, it gets better. When the Lord and Moses start to talk over the situation, Moses dumps all of his frustration at God's feet (11:10–15). I suppose this is not surprising, since—after all—Moses was a re-luctant leader, called by God from a burning bush to bring God's people out of Egypt (Ex. 3).

So, upon hearing the peoples' wailing, Moses cuts loose—pointing out that he is not their father, implying that they are acting like a bunch of babies, skeptical that their request can be granted, and then, asking to be killed, if this treatment continues. Surely we are dealing with someone who was not prepared for what he was facing! After being coached all the way through the plagues in Egypt, with Aaron as his assistant, Moses still does not want to have to put up with all this mess from the people.

Finally, the LORD gets a chance to reply—in the text quoted at the beginning of this chapter. First, God arranges to distribute some of Moses' responsibilities—"the burden of the people" (Num. 11:17c)—to some of Israel's elders and officers. Then the matter of the request for meat is addressed. Moses is instructed to tell the people their request will be granted. They will get meat, and they are expected to eat it. Not only this, but God says that the people must eat meat every day for a month, until they get sick of it! They will eat meat until "it comes out of [their] nostrils" (Num. 11:20b). The reason for this sickening indulgence is not left to conjecture: God finishes the instructions to Moses by interpreting the people's wailing as a lack of faith. In spite of their deliverance from Egypt, and the nourishment of manna in the wilderness, the Israelites' words and actions tell the story of their state of mind. They are not trusting God's promise. In response, the LORD tells Moses, "Now you shall see whether my word will come true for you or not" (Num. 11:23b).

Surely, we cannot downplay the gravity of this story. Throughout the ongoing narrative in the Hebrew Bible, the people's wavering trust in and devotion to their exodus savior leads to all sorts of tragic consequences. This point comes across in one generation of Israelites after another, in one biblical book after another. We do not want to make light of this message.

However, let us not allow awareness of this sober biblical theme to overshadow, in this one particular story, a remarkable and provocative quality. There is some humor—is there not?—in God's telling the people they will eat so much meat it will come out of their nostrils. The image is a vivid one; it reminds George of a scene at home, growing up with three brothers, at the kitchen table, giggling uncontrollably over some impropriety about food and eating. Social norms about food can lead to some downright funny, even a little bawdy, scenarios. Surely, we can appreciate the ancient storyteller using humor in this subtle way to emphasize a serious point.

The God of the Hebrew Scriptures has a sense of humor—even in the midst of circumstances and events that the called ones dare not forget.

This story from Numbers 11 speaks so clearly to the theme of this book. The events recounted occur in a major chapter of in-between time. The Israelites' wilderness wanderings comprise a series of experiences that occurred between two major events of their Big Story. As we already have noted, the first major event was Israel's release from captivity in Egypt, as the slaves of Pharaoh. Second was their entry into the Promised Land, the place where all twelve tribes received allotments of land as everlasting inheritances. Yet more than once our spiritual ancestors in the Scriptures found themselves in between—not where they used to be anymore, but not yet where they would end up.

We are not that different from our spiritual ancestors, are we? Although we do not like to admit it, we understand this tendency to turn our backs on God when times get tough. Our churches sometimes act just like the ancient Israelites, complaining and wailing when we don't get our way. Oh, we never would want to imagine that it was because we were not trusting God. Yet, throughout this book, the two of us are seeking to help you and your church claim the reality of in-between times—and then to learn to live into them. In this final chapter, then, we see the story of "meat out of your nostrils" serving as one more biblical metaphor for a congregational challenge of spirit.

In-between times stimulate new possibilities, which in turn create resistance. It is the purpose of this chapter to prepare you to respond to resistance, understanding it as a normal and natural part of your journey. Our interpretation of Numbers 11 suggests that resistance can be managed more effectively if we approach it with good-natured humor. Learning to chuckle at ourselves in the midst of our transitions is not only good for us psychologically; there are also hints in the Scriptures of its spiritual efficacy.

Resistance can be managed if we approach it with
good-natured humor!

Do Not Disturb

As we consider this matter of handling resistance constructively, the two of us remember a sign we saw in our hotel while we were attending a large conference. Most hotels supply every room with a doorknob hanger that typically says, "Do Not Disturb." Hung on the outside door of your room, this sign's purpose is to alert the housekeeping crew if you do not want them to visit your room. At this particular hotel, the two of us were walking the hallways when we noticed that the wording on this hotel's doorknob hanger was unlike any that we ever had seen. It said: "No Surprises Please—Do Not Disturb." We looked at each other for a moment and then began to chuckle, for we were thinking the same thing: What an apt slogan for churches that are not yet ready to face their in-between times!

In a book that treats transition as an inevitable part of a church's journey of faith, it is necessary to talk about congregational resistance. All the best-laid plans will avail nothing if they do not account for the realities of resistance. Any organization whose context experiences significant change will be tempted to behave as if it can continue with business as usual and still remain effective. On this point, religious congregations are no different. Churches sometimes persist with the same activities and procedures for a long time, in spite of glaring evidence that they are losing effectiveness. Not only this, congregations sometimes engage in behaviors of resistance that outsiders would view as odd, even harmful.

In our seminary teaching, we have found the insights of Edgar Schein to be very applicable to religious settings.[2] Schein has spent a career helping businesses understand their cultures and how to undertake change processes realistically and productively. His ideas about how organizations "un-learn" old ways and then learn new things strike us as right on target for churches. We believe that you will discover, in our discussion of Schein that follows, a host of useful—and sometimes profound—tools that will open a way for the surprising movement of grace in your midst.

Schein begins his discussion of learning and change by emphasizing that adults learn differently than children. Unlike children, he says, adults often must begin the learning process by *un*-learning.[3] Children are learning everything for the first time, while adults already have learned many things. This backlog of experience, Schein suggests, often gets in the way of adults and new learning. For example, think about how quickly children learn to use the latest electronic devices. Even when we adults want to learn these new technologies, our brains can take longer to do so. The neurological patterns already in place actually can hinder our learning something new. In this kind of situation, resistance emerges, even in spite of our interest and efforts.

Imagine, then, what resistance might look like when we are *not* trying to learn.[4] If a person or group perceives that a new proposal will mean that they have to stop doing something with which they are comfortable, they might refuse to do it. They might oppose, defy, undermine, or seek some other way to prevent the proposal from being adopted. Resistance, then, is based sometimes on will, other times on capability: In other words, sometimes people don't want to change; other times, they don't know how to change. Either way, we can see that—for a community in transition—resistance should be treated as a normal reaction.

Schein also says that resistance will be particularly strong if members of the organization perceive (even dimly) that a possible change will mean giving up some of their deeply held beliefs. Perhaps some new members visit a church board meeting, requesting a contemporary worship service with guitars and percussion or seeking to set up a crosstown vacation Bible school to help a new church of a different ethnic heritage. Any such idea or request becomes a new, proposed artifact (or set of artifacts) for the congregation's cultural pond. Proposed new artifacts potentially disrupt the church's stability, the equilibrium which also acts to filter the large amounts of data the church encounters in the world around it.[5]

Ideas for new artifacts are fragile: They don't necessarily go anywhere. By contrast, submerged beliefs contain a group's deepest energies—and they will not go down without some effort . These unconscious, unquestioned principles represent what the organization "feels in its bones" about how to make sense out of the world, what gives it order, what to expect. No wonder resistance is so strong. It is hard to give up deeply held beliefs that are mostly unconscious.

*Resistance will be strong. It is hard to give up deeply
held beliefs that are mostly unconscious.*

On the other hand, we live in a world that rarely lets anyone or anything sit still for long. Schein argues that adults will not learn to deal with change (and transition always prompts change of some kind) unless something comes along that disturbs the status quo. We love our routines, our familiar schedules, our comfortable patterns! Unless we pay attention to whatever information or factors could upset our applecart, we will not see a need for doing anything differently. Schein refers to these upsetting indicators as "disconfirming forces." They can take on a number of appearances,[6] but what they have in common is delivering "bad news." Ironically, organizational learning begins only when whatever is viewed as bad news is heard and acknowledged.

So what happens to a church when some individual, some group, or some network of members says that it sees disconfirming forces? Church finances have been dropping for five years; the number of teenagers involved in youth ministry activities is half of what it was three years ago; the pastor resigns suddenly and no one seems to know why; the sixty-year-old boiler breaks down again, and this time it cannot be repaired. Any or all of these occurrences might be signs that a church is entering a time of transition. To understand any in-between time, we learn to pay attention not simply to the details on the surface. We ask ourselves, in a nonthreatening way, what the circumstances in question suggest about where the congregation is right now. What disconfirming forces are delivering important news that we do not want to hear?

Learning how to ask a question like this one takes a calm presence in the midst of potential chaos. To this point, Schein helps us name yet another part of our reality in the in-between—namely, that disconfirmation triggers anxiety. Understanding the nature of anxiety, and learning how to manage it, is a vital key to dealing with resistance productively. So we need to spend some time in this chapter looking at anxiety more deeply. Ignoring anxiety is perilous, but allowing it to run amok in your church is even more certain to do harm.

*Understanding the nature of anxiety, and learning
how to manage it, is a vital key to dealing with
resistance productively.*

Understanding and Managing Anxiety

As an organizational psychologist, Schein realizes that group anxiety takes two forms that need to be understood in relationship to each other. The first kind of anxiety that a group experiences Schein calls "survival anxiety." What happens when disconfirming information about something in your church is not ignored or denied? How will those who acknowledge the truth of this information feel and react? Even when it is not expressed in words, people will feel uncomfortable.[7] Church members and staff alike will be wondering what might happen to the church if this matter is not faced. Survival anxiety is a feeling of wondering, "Can we make it? If we don't do anything about our current situation, will we survive in the long run?" Regardless of how and where this moment of naming the truth occurs, the reaction will be survival anxiety.[8] Even if the church is not facing its imminent demise, survival anxiety in these circumstances is natural, normal, and—yes—necessary.

However, simply acknowledging the truth about your church's situation will not get you through your in-between time. There is a danger that a second form of anxiety could leave you feeling stuck, unable to move. This second form is what Shein calls "learning anxiety." A church dominated by learning anxiety is a bit like Chicken Little running around the barnyard and screeching, "The sky is falling!" but failing to do anything to help himself or anyone else. Learning anxiety can paralyze a congregation as surely as denial of the disconfirming forces. This is because members and staff might be afraid that listening to these forces will call for a kind of response that they cannot or will not do.

What do such fears look like? Of those that Schein names, three are easy to understand in a congregational context:[9]

1. The fear that your standing and influence will disappear
Imagine that your pastor retires after fifteen years at your church. During her pastoral tenure, a cadre of ten church members has enjoyed a cordial and effective working affiliation with her. In their own ways, each one has liked this situation, because it gave them privileged opportunities. Some of these church members liked to promote their own ideas as major decisions were considered. Others enjoyed being known

by other members as someone who was capable, trustworthy, and reliable. Still others saw the special relationship with the pastor as implied permission for their own pet projects. These church members now wonder: What will happen to my status when a new pastor arrives?

2. The fear that a new direction or emphasis will not fulfill you

Employees of companies that are sold or taken over by another corporation know what it is like to wonder what their jobs will become once the takeover is complete. It is common for congregations to lose members when a pastor leaves, when the church moves locations, when a major new ministry is undertaken, after an internal scandal, or in the wake of other significant changes. How might you feel if the new thing that comes next in the life of your congregation appears not to match what you believe or prefer?

3. The fear that you won't fit in anymore

One reason people join congregations is to belong. Churches develop various networks of people with common interests and commitments; over the years, these networks can be very nurturing, as well as useful to the church. The awareness of entering an in-between time can trigger among members some uncertainty about whether the conditions that sustain those commitments will remain. What if some of your church friends and partners in ministry don't share your perspective on possible changes? What if you start feeling left out of events, gatherings, and activities that have meant so much to you?

Fear is real, and fear is natural—but it also needs to be managed. Part of the grace in any in-between journey comes in the awareness that there will be periods of being unsettled. We can expect such moments to trigger behavior that could (and probably will) distract the congregation. Since fear creates resistance, it is important to know how to handle it constructively. We start, then, with awareness—awareness of these two kinds of anxiety and how they correlate.

On this critical point, Schein again is very insightful. He describes the relationship between survival anxiety and learning anxiety with two pithy but pregnant statements.[10] The first one says that, in order for an organization to move forward in a time of transition, the concern for "making it" has to be stronger than the fears involved in figuring out what to do. In Schein's words:

"Survival anxiety . . . must be greater than learning anxiety."

Schein's second principle addresses how the first principle needs to be maintained:

"Learning anxiety must be reduced rather than increasing survival anxiety."

In other words, whatever action is taken needs to help the church members and staff feel more confident about what they are doing. Trying to motivate the congregation by "gloom-and-doom" tactics will backfire. Schein makes it clear: Any change process will be effective only as group members feel that they are getting a handle on the kinds of actions and conduct that will help their group succeed. In other words, the learning anxiety has to be eased. As long as the concern for surviving is evident, a congregation that is working on—and trying out—new plans will be on its way.

Ensuring Psychological Safety

So, what does it take for a church to follow these two principles? Schein emphasizes that those overseeing the transition must take seriously the need for everyone in the organization to have "psychological safety."[11] By this, Schein means that tactics are employed to bolster group members' sense that both their discomfort and their efforts will be worth it. The pastor, other staff, and church board need to work together to demonstrate to the entire congregation their own commitment to the journey. This commitment will require a focused and sustained investment of time, energy, and appropriate resources.

Psychological safety takes several forms, and all of them require attention. For communities of faith, the first one might seem obvious— but it is ignored at the congregation's peril:

1. *A spiritual and theological rationale and support for in-between times*

Pastors are trained in Bible, history, theology, and ethics to function as the congregation's practical theologian. Preaching, community prayers, study groups, and devotional moments all become occasions in the rhythm of a congregation's life when the pastor is looked to as a spiritual leader. During in-between times, these moments dare not be overlooked. The pastor has a key role in framing transition with appropriate biblical, theological, and spiritual images and sayings (see the next paragraph). But the two of us do not believe the pastor should work alone in this task. Hopefully, elders, deacons, and board members can contribute as well. However, a pastor needs to be ready to bring clarity, encouragement, and comfort to a congregation, especially in a season of transition.

For instance, what preaching theme would be fitting and helpful for a congregation just now acknowledging that its lifecycle phase is weakening? Handled sensitively, sermons from the "dry bones" chapter in Ezekiel (37:1–14) or texts from the exile ("Comfort, O comfort my people, says your God. Speak tenderly to Jerusalem, and cry to her that she has served her term," Isa. 40:1–2) can help the congregation see its current situation anew in light of the shifting circumstances of our biblical ancestors. A Bible study on the wilderness stories in the Pentateuch can help church members discuss parallels between the Israelites' behavior and their own. In such a study, there is plenty of room around the table for honest, good-hearted laughter! When we can laugh at ourselves in a safe space, our learning anxiety can stay manageable.

Your church's theological emphasis during transition does not necessarily have to sound unfamiliar. Many congregations are part of denominations or traditions that emphasize certain doctrines and practices. Often a revisiting of these traditions can stimulate ideas for appropriating them in new ways for a new day. We encourage such revisiting and use of results that it can generate.

Similarly, your transition theology should leave enough room for an eventual clarity of vision. The congregation traveling through in-between times needs to double-check its vision: What is it? How clear is it? How appropriate is this refreshed vision to the current situation? How well is it being followed? Remember, the further into lifecycle decline your church is, the more essential it is to revisit vision.[12]

At the same time, however, words of assurance can go only so far by themselves. The famous twentieth-century mathematician and philosopher Alfred North Whitehead once said, "The vitality of thought is in adventure. . . . Ideas won't keep. Something must be done about them."[13] Pastors learn quickly enough that the uplifting theological ideas presented in studies and sermons must "have feet"—or the congregation won't know how to do something about them. This awareness helps explain a second task in providing psychological safety for the congregation in transition:

2. Engagement of the congregation

A church's response in transition will go nowhere unless the congregation is involved and engaged. In this respect, most North American churches are somewhat different from businesses. In a business, changes in goals and procedures can be imposed on employees, who are expected to "get with the program" or find another job. In a congregation, a strictly hierarchical approach does not make sense. It risks alienating members, especially if most of them have not been given an opportunity to participate in discussions, decisions, and actions regarding the transitional challenges. What works better in the long run is for members to be fully involved, using processes that fit the congregation's form of governance. This kind of inclusion is not difficult to undertake in smaller churches, many of which are quietly aware of their stagnation. Even in larger congregations, however, focus groups and cottage meetings can be held to interpret circumstances, air questions and fears, and brainstorm initial ideas. One of the best ways to ensure that the transition will hurt your church is to avoid talking about it.

3. Preparation for taking on the decisions and tasks ahead

There is a tendency in American life to move quickly when uncertainty looms, to act decisively in order to quell fears. This popular style dominates adventure films even today, but it is a poor model for churches in transition! Most in-between times have more at stake and require more energy than it takes to mow your lawn or repaint the kitchen. In other words, don't approach transition as a routine to rush through, or your church will find itself wrestling again and again with the issues that prompted the transition in the first place.

A congregation in the in-between times
needs to double-check its vision.

In-between times offer the perceptive congregation a time to re-affirm its spiritual grounding. This is a time to take a deep breath, to acknowledge anxieties, and then to give some collective time for the congregation to pay attention to itself. Perhaps a study series, a retreat, or a field trip to mission sites of interest will do the trick. Along the way, there will some new insights and skills for you to learn—about your neighborhood, about changes in the generations, about the people nearby who are different from your church members in some way, about resources that might help your church.

This third form of psychological safety—preparing for decisions and tasks—addresses the need to shift into learning mode. There will be moments when your church might feel as if what it is learning is not focused or relevant enough. That is the way that our grade-school children feel about arithmetic! It is true: We cannot always see the value of something when we are learning it for the first time. Nonetheless, learning more about your congregation, its changing context, and new ideas to test out is essential preparation for your church's journey of faith.

4. Opportunities to try out new ideas, be supported, and assess their effectiveness

Discussions and learning experiences are not the only way members need to be involved in their church's in-between times. Whatever courses of action are chosen, they should involve as wide a swath of members as possible. If our view of "church" has something to do with a community called forth to give witness to God's claims on the world, then in-between times become the work of the people. The pastor and a few key members might think about and discuss the transition more than others, but the work of the journey cannot be theirs alone.

What kinds of activities and projects would not require too much time and energy but represent commitment to your "grace for the journey"? How can these efforts be undertaken and then reviewed? A rhythm of action and reflection helps create an environment that will be essential for guiding your church's transition.

5. Modeling by the pastor, staff, church officers, and other key members.

During in-between times, those persons who hold positions of authority bear a significant responsibility. The rest of the congregation will see them as representing the new emphasis or direction that is emerging. Churches expect their pastors, staff members, and officers to inspire and lead the way; that is one of their most important tasks. Your congregation must be able to see in their words and deeds that all of these officials are putting their money where their mouth is.

Additionally, in every congregation there are persons of influence whose opinions and actions sway other members. These "key culture bearers"[14] will need to be on board early in any transition process, just as they will have been part of receiving any bad news that led to it. Key culture bearers are often the individuals who are most associated with the church as it is; in a sense, they have the most to lose during in-between times. So it is essential that the congregation believes these influential church members are giving the transitional journey their trust and support.

What we are talking about here is integrity. If the congregation is to trust that its response to transition will be both worthwhile and effective, members must be able to see that response in key culture bearers, the pastor, the deacons, the elders, and other officers. This does not mean, however, that these key people need to pretend everything is fine all of the time. Rather, as officers and influential members share their own moments of uncertainty and their struggles with change, members receive assurance. What sustains your church during this time transcends any one person or group; it is the shared conviction that a new chapter of ministry and mission is about to emerge.

In many respects, key culture bearers
have the most to lose.

6. *New internal processes that go along with the new ideas being developed*

The last form that psychological safety takes for a church in transition might seem odd or unnecessary, but it is not. Resistance to change can be fueled if members of the organization do not see any real differences in the way that the group conducts its business. One of the easiest places to demonstrate the church's internal commitment to transition is in the method and content of communication. Church members need to be able to hear and see that the journey is on its way. They need to receive updates on particular elements of the process and opportunities to have their questions answered appropriately. When reports and conversations about the changes become common in your church's public arena, learning anxiety is reduced substantially.

A church's communication efforts can also draw positive attention to members and groups whose activities personify the new directions the church is pursuing. Genuine praise for a "short-term win"[15] not only gives credit where credit is due; it also provides the congregation with a helpful example of where the journey is headed and what the "new thing" is shaping up to look like. Hearing the stories of one new success might inspire the ideas of other members.

Sometimes a transitional journey prompts the congregation to simplify its organizational structure.[16] George once consulted with a congregation in transition that had decided to streamline its operations and reduce the number of meetings. Its solution was to reorganize with only three committees, which were named simply "Us" (in-house ministry matters), "Them" (mission and outreach), and "Stuff" (property, finance, operations, etc.). The streamlining freed the congregation to imagine more openly about its purpose and to align its activities with that purpose. Reducing internal structure and red tape allows a congregation to focus more of its energy on big-picture issues.

Let's review the essential elements that provide psychological safety for a church during its in-between time:

1. A spiritual and theological rationale and support for in-between times;
2. Engagement of the congregation;
3. Preparation for taking on the decisions and tasks ahead;
4. Opportunities to try out new ideas, be supported, and assess their effectiveness;
5. Modeling by the pastor, staff, church officers, and other key members; and
6. New internal processes that go along with the new ideas being developed.

All of these factors will help the congregation overcome its normal and natural resistance. By taking them in order, and maintaining each one even as the next one is begun, a congregation positions itself for grace-filled discoveries.

Along the way, the two of us also hope that something else will happen. We hope that your congregation will realize that is has learned how to deal with transition, any transition. Rather than mimicking the Israelites who complained to Moses about their circumstances, your congregation will be gaining spiritual wisdom. Rather than fighting tooth and nail against the leading of the Spirit, your congregation will have learned something about living with uncertainty. It is a profound lesson, one that few churches allow themselves to encounter. When they do, however, they discover that the journey itself becomes a blessing. Then, as they laugh together in joy, they bear witness to a God who works with and through us, just as God finds us—with our foibles, our resistance, and all.

Spiritual Practice

What would it be like to imagine God as the Stillpoint of your in-between time?

"Be still, and know that I am God."

—Psalm 46:10

Your *guide* for this practice will invite you into this time of reflection as follows:

As you gather in your circle again, take a deep breath and slowly breathe out.

Repeat this breathing exercise three times. Then, sit in silence for a few minutes.

Quietly and slowly, your *guide* will invite you to reflect silently on two questions:

1. What is your Stillpoint?
2. To what do you cling when you need direction?

Guide: As you silently reflect on these questions, invite members of the circle to begin to read, one by one, the phrases of the psalm as written below. Individuals do not have to go around the circle in order. Just begin as you feel led and let the psalmist's words flow.

Be still . . .
Be still and know . . .
Be still and know that I am . . . God.

Center your hearts and minds in these words as you continue to sit in silence. Then the *guide* will invite you to meditate again on this question:

What would it be like to imagine God as the Stillpoint of your congregation's journey?

Live into the silence until you feel ready to share your reply.

Be sure to listen to one another without question or comment.

Encourage everyone to share, but do not require that every person do so.

After everyone has spoken and your time together draws to a close, pray together, thanking God for guidance in the midst of uncertainty.

Afterword

When we moved to the mountains of North Georgia several years ago, our family, friends, and colleagues all assumed we did it to get away from the hectic pace of city life. Actually, George had long missed living where he could see mountains, since he had lived near them for many years out West. For Beverly, the move meant coming full circle, returning home to her Cherokee and Appalachian roots. So even though George is on faculty at a theological school in Atlanta, we decided to make the sixty-five-mile move to this wonderful, historic farmhouse we now call home.

About the time we closed on the farmhouse, the bottom fell out of the real estate market. So there we were, sitting with two mortgage payments, wondering how this could ever work out. But we waited, actively.

Over time, we moved more and more furniture to the house in the mountains and repainted wall after wall in our house in Atlanta, hoping that spacious-looking rooms and fresh paint somehow would attract a buyer. Even as we continued to wait for our house in Atlanta to sell, we spent as much time as we could in the mountains. One of the unusual delights of this 1878 farmhouse is that it sits hardly a stone's throw from the Etowah River and is surrounded by many species of native wildflowers.

On each visit to the house that first summer and fall, we were surprised to behold yet another abundant display of unfamiliar yet stunning blossoms. One very tall row of bushes, however, looked gangly and unkempt, out of place in this yard of old trees and antique rosebushes. George made a mental note that those bushes easily could be cut out—in the spring, when we had more time.

You can imagine, then, our bewilderment the following spring when we discovered that the huge "shrubs" we intended to cut down were setting up a loaded crop of something. It took only a brief inspection to realize we were looking at a double row of mature blueberry bushes. This unexpected discovery dumbfounded us at first—but then we got excited! That summer, although the bushes required a stepladder and the inside canes twisted around one another like vines in a fairy tale, we savored every handful of the dark blue, sweet-yet-tart berries. Bags of washed berries ended up in the freezer, to be eaten on cereal in the winter and given to family and friends. We were so pleased and grateful that someone decades before us had planted and nurtured those bushes, so that we could now enjoy and share their healthy fruit.

This summer, in order to continue working on this book, we decided to get away from all the demands that called to us on our small farm. Before leaving home, we picked all the ripe blueberries we could gather, so the birds would not feast on them while we were gone. When we arrived back home a week later, we could not help but notice that the berries waiting to be picked were much larger and sweeter than the ones we had picked earlier. Aha! We finally understood—in order to have the sweetest, most delightful berries, we needed to wait until their time, not ours.

It was yet another reminder—waiting makes the difference.

Throughout this book, we have shared with you images, biblical reflections, directional signs, spiritual practices, and cultural frameworks. All these features have been designed to help you and your congregation claim its in-between time in a positive and life-giving way. You have discovered by now that this is not a "how-to" book as much as a "why-to" book. That is, we have not provided you with a step-by-step manual to follow, as though living through transition can be managed like changing out a water faucet. Rather, the challenge with in-between times is recognizing how they trigger deep congregational realities that are both spiritual and cultural. The textures of this kind of fabric are unfamiliar territory for most of us.

We encourage and invite you and your congregation to reflect now and again on the images and photographs used in the chapters. They can serve to remind you that, on this journey of witness to faith, you will have lots of stops, twists, and turns. At times, you and your congregation may find yourselves looking in various directions, seeking to discern the right way. Sometimes you will need to say "whoa!" and pay careful attention to what is going on, in the church and in the world around you.

We hope that road signs like these will serve as vivid reminders: As your church journeys through transition, remember to pay attention to those things that can give you a sense of direction.

Make no mistake: Learning to living faithfully through transition is not like selecting paint colors for the Sunday school rooms or choosing a theme park for the next middle school outing. Unless churches are willing to claim the in-between time as a place of new promise, they will miss connecting with those persons or groups of people in their midst who are seeking fresh new expressions of faith. We cannot imagine God's call on our common life in new ways without in-between times.

So, within the many rhythms of life and faith, we offer you here a special kind of companionship. With this kind of company, on this kind of journey, may you truly discover grace.

Notes

INTRODUCTION

1. The idea of "practices" has become a significant part of current conversations on Christian life and identity. See Dorothy C. Bass, editor, *Practicing Our Faith: A Way of Life for a Searching People* (San Francisco: Jossey-Bass, 1997); and Diana Butler Bass, *The Practicing Congregation: Imagining a New Old Church* (Herndon, VA: The Alban Institute, 2004).

CHAPTER 1: FINDING YOURSELF IN THE IN-BETWEEN

1. Rodney Clapp, "Eugene Peterson: A Monk Out of Habit," *Christianity Today,* April 3, 1987, 25.
2. The concept of "liminality" has a long history in cultural anthropology and is a very helpful image for churches. Liminality describes the middle stage of a rite of passage, the period in which one has left one's familiar, structured world but has not yet entered a new reality. It describes a time that is "betwixt and between"— no longer what it was previously but not yet something new and definite. The concepts and theory of rites of passage originate with Arnold van Gennep and have been utilized extensively in anthropological literature. Victor Turner extended van Gennep's work to see liminality at work in human communities of many kinds, including churches and church movements. For a summary of these ideas, see Nigel Rapport and Joanna Overing, *Social and Cultural Anthropology: The Key Concepts* (London and New York: Routledge, 2000), 229–235.

3. The concept of "communitas" was developed by Victor Turner, who built upon the ideas of Arnold van Gennep about rites of passage (see note 2). See Rapport and Overing, *Social and Cultural Anthropology,* 233–235.

4. See Beverly A. Brigman (Thompson), "Seeking God in the Midst of Transition," unpublished D.Min. dissertation (Decatur, GA: Columbia Theological Seminary, 2000).

5. Robert Kegan, *The Evolving Self* (Cambridge: Harvard University Press, 1982), 125; as cited in Brigman, "Seeking God in the Midst of Transition," 18.

6. Dorothy C. Bass and Craig Dykstra, editors, *Practicing Our Faith: A Way of Life for a Searching People* (San Francisco: Jossey-Bass, 1997), 6.

7. Dorothy Bass, *Practicing Our Faith,* 7.

8. See Diana Butler Bass, *The Practicing Congregation: Imagining a New Old Church* (Herndon, VA: The Alban Institute, 2004).

CHAPTER 2: NAMING YOUR ENERGY

1. The cultural approach embedded in this book is one George B. Thompson, Jr. developed and has discussed in two of his earlier books: *How to Get Along with Your Church: Creating Cultural Capital for Doing Ministry* (Cleveland: The Pilgrim Press, 2001); and *How to Get Along with Your Pastor: Creating Partnership for Doing Ministry* (Cleveland: The Pilgrim Press, 2006).

2. These three distinct types of cultural framing are mentioned, and then elaborated on in Part One of *How to Get Along with Your Pastor,* xxiv–xv.

3. Using a slightly different metaphor—that of a swamp—the model laid out in this chapter may be found elaborated in *How to Get Along with Your Pastor,* chapter 1.

4. This term "key culture bearers" describes "persons who have gained sufficient cultural capital to be recognized as standing for the well-being of the congregation and speaking for what it most treasures." See *How to Get Along with Your Pastor,* xv.

5. The phrase "a sense of urgency" is most readily identified with an organizational change process that John Kotter spells out in

Leading Change (Boston: Harvard Business School Press, 1996). See his discussion in chapter 3, "Establishing a Sense of Urgency."

CHAPTER 3: COCOONS AND THE INTERNET

1. Sue Monk Kidd, *When the Heart Waits* (San Francisco: Harper Collins, 1990), 12–15.
2. See George B. Thompson, Jr.'s explanation of confluence theory in *How to Get Along with Your Pastor: Creating Partnership for Doing Ministry* (Cleveland: The Pilgrim Press, 2006), chapter 3. The discussion here is drawn from this chapter.
3. Generational theory has been widely discussed in the literature, especially of late in higher education, to anticipate generational factors that could influence the way in which young college students learn. The primary source for generational theory has been William Strauss and Neil Howe's *Generations: The History of America's Future, 1584–2069* (New York: William Morrow, 1991). A simpler version of generational theory, independently developed, was published a few years earlier for a church audience; it is Douglas Walrath, *Frameworks: Patterns for Living and Believing Today* (Cleveland: The Pilgrim Press, 1987).
4. A short but helpful discussion of oral culture and its relevance for pastoral ministry is found in Tex Sample, *Ministry in an Oral Culture: Living with Will Rogers, Uncle Remus, and Minnie Pearl* (Louisville: Westminster John Knox Press, 1994).
5. Trina Paulus, words and pictures, *Hope for the Flowers* (New York: Paulist Press/A Newman Book, 1972).
6. Ibid., 75.
7. Ibid., 76.

CHAPTER 4: DIGGING EVEN DEEPER

1. A discussion of external and internal organizational issues is spelled out clearly in Edgar Schein, *Organizational Culture and Leadership,* 3rd edition (San Francisco: Jossey-Bass, 2004), chapter 5, "Assumptions about External Adaptation Issues," (mission and strategy, goals, means, measurement, and correction) and

chapter 6, "Assumptions about Managing Internal Integration" (common language and conceptual categories; group boundaries; power and status; norms of intimacy, friendship, and love; rewards and punishments; explaining the unexplainable).

2. This set of ideas was explained in chapter 3 under the terms "confluence" and "streams of culture."

3. Amish communities in the United States offer a fascinating example of this point. As they have sought for many generations to maintain their traditional religious practices and "old-fashioned" way of economic and social life, Amish have developed ways of adapting that appear to the rest of us to be both odd and creative. For a sympathetic but fair sociological analysis, see Donald Kraybill, *The Riddle of Amish Culture*, revised edition (Baltimore: The Johns Hopkins University Press, 2001).

4. See references to this research in Schein, *Organizational Culture and Leadership*, chapters 7–9.

5. See Schein, *Organizational Culture and Leadership*, 151–163; see also George B. Thompson Jr.'s *How to Get Along with Your Pastor: Creating Partnership for Doing Ministry* (Cleveland: The Pilgrim Press, 2006), 8–9.

6. See Schein, *Organizational Culture and Leadership*, 163–170, especially 164–165.

7. See Schein, *Organizational Culture and Leadership*, chapter 9, especially 178–187.

8. Mark Lau Branson, *Memories, Hopes, and Conversations: Appreciative Inquiry and Congregational Change* (Herndon, VA: The Alban Institute, 2004).

CHAPTER 5: DISCOVERING TREASURE

1. These four phases are also discussed in George B. Thompson Jr.'s book, *How to Get Along with Your Pastor: Creating Partnership for Doing Ministry*, (Cleveland: The Pilgrim Press, 2006), chapter 2.

2. For the purposes of this book, we are presenting a version of the lifecycle model that is simpler than models available in other literature. The lifecycle model we have found most helpful was

published by Ichak Adizes in his book *Corporate Lifecycles: How and Why Corporations Grow and Die and What to Do About It* (Englewood Cliffs, NJ: Prentice Hall, 1988), which George B. Thompson, Jr. adapted for his book *How to Get Along with Your Pastor.*

3. See Robert Wuthnow's discussion in *After the Baby Boomers: How Twenty- and Thirty-Somethings Are Shaping the Future of American Religion* (Princeton: Princeton University Press, 2007).

4. A discussion of the four organizational functions that are mentioned in this paragraph and chapter can be found in Thompson, Jr., *How to Get Along with Your Pastor,* chapter 2, pp. 22ff.

5. The discussion part of this spiritual practice is adapted from Eric Law, *The Wolf Shall Dwell with the Lamb: A Spirituality for Leadership in a Multicultural Community* (St. Louis: Chalice Press, 1993), chapter 9, "Mutual Invitation as Mutual Empowerment."

CHAPTER 6: NO SURPRISES PLEASE

1. The word translated "complain" in verse 1 is rare in the Hebrew Bible, used only here and in Lamentations 3:39. Similarly, the word translated "rabble" in Numbers 11:4 is found nowhere else in the Bible. See Thomas B. Dozeman, *The New Interpreter's Bible, Vol. II* (Nashville: Abingdon Press, 1998), 104–105. These observations suggest a unique source for the story, but certainly not an unusual point about the attitude and behavior of the Israelites.

2. Edgar Schein, *The Corporate Culture Survival Guide,* revised edition (San Francisco: Jossey-Bass, 2009), especially chapter 6.

3. Schein, *The Corporate Culture Survival Guide,* 105.

4. Ibid.

5. Ibid., 105–106.

6. Ibid., 107.

7. Ibid., 111.

8. This idea of the church naming the truth about itself is discussed in George B. Thompson, Jr., *How to Get Along with Your Church: Creating Capital for Doing Ministry* (Cleveland: The Pilgrim Press, 2001), chapter 4; see especially page 68.

9. Schein, *The Corporate Culture Survival Guide,* 112–113.

10. Ibid., 114–115.

11. Schein's explanation of psychological safety and the eight steps necessary to maintain it in a corporate context are found in *The Corporate Culture Survival Guide*, 115–117. For our purposes in this book, we are abbreviating his list.

12. Resources for helping congregations discern fresh vision can be found in the literature. See Lovett Weems' useful discussion of vision in his book *Church Leadership: Vision, Culture, Team, Integrity*, revised edition (Nashville: Abingdon Press, 2009), chapter. 2. See also George B. Thompson, Jr., *Futuring Your Church: Finding Your Vision and Making It Work* (Cleveland: The Pilgrim Press, 1999).

13. Alfred North Whitehead, recorded by Lucien Price, *Dialogues of Alfred North Whitehead* (New York: Mentor Books, 1956), 205.

14. This term is introduced and used in George B. Thompson, Jr., *How to Get Along with Your Church*, p. 68, and is utilized also in *How to Get Along with Your Pastor*, pp. 88, 103–104.

15. John Kotter emphasizes the value of short-term wins to an organizational change process. See his book *Leading Change* (Boston: Harvard Business School Press, 1996), chapter 8.

16. Organizational consultant Ichak Adizes explains the value of structural streamlining in his book, *Corporate Lifecycles: How and Why Corporations Grow and Die and What to Do About It* (Englewood Cliffs, NJ: Prentice Hall, 1988). See his discussion of "decentralization" on pp. 338–339.